Basic Millinery for the Stage

Basic Millinery for the Stage

Tim Dial

Heinemann
Portsmouth, NH

Heinemann
361 Hanover Street
Portsmouth, NH 03801–3912
www.heinemanndrama.com

Offices and agents throughout the world

Library of Congress Cataloging-in-Publication Data
Dial, Tim.
    Basic millinery for the stage / Tim Dial.
        p.   cm.
    Includes bibliographical references.
        ISBN 0-325-00336-X (pbk. : alk. paper)
    1. Millinery. I. Title.
    PN2067 .D53 2002
    792'.026—dc21   2002001578

Editor: Lisa A. Barnett
Production: Lynne Reed
Manufacturing: Steve Bernier
Cover design: Night & Day Design
Typesetter: Publishers' Design and Production Services, Inc.
Text photographer: Tim Dial
Models: Melanie Starnes-Mortimer and Allison Steadman
Photo lab supervisor: Melanie Starnes-Mortimer

Printed in the United States of America on acid-free paper
Docutech RRD 2011

Contents

Contents

Acknowledgments

Thanks to Laura McCammon, who got me into this line of work. Also, thanks to Marianne Custer, L.J. and Mari DeCuir, Anne Knight, Marcia Goldenstein, Melanie Starnes-Mortimer, Allison Steadman, Margaret Reese, and Roy and Linda Dial. Thank you, Jeff Lieder, and all of the gang at the Utah Shakespearean Festival. And thanks to the many craftspeople I have had the pleasure to work with over the years.

And a very special thank you to Bill Black.

Introduction

In the early 1980s I was asked to make my first hat. It had never occurred to me that hats were things that got made. I suppose I had never considered hats much at all. The show was *The Importance of Being Earnest*, and the hats were large, Victorian, and very decorated, so I looked for some guidelines to help me through the process—something to tell me where I should start. But I couldn't find anything, and had to make up a process as I went along. Since then I have learned a lot, met a lot of hatmakers, and found that I was not alone in my frustration. Many theatrical hatmakers have had very informal training, or formal training that emphasized clothing construction with little millinery instruction. Now that I teach college, I have searched for a book that would help me teach my students the many techniques and basic principles of millinery in a clear, concise way—but the search has largely been in vain. So I have made my own. In this text I specifically approach millinery for the theater, introducing basic techniques and broader ideas that serve as a foundation for more advanced techniques and more difficult projects.

So how do you become a good milliner? Like fine tailoring, millinery uses many standard sewing techniques, along with other specialized technical skills. I suggest that students learn basic sewing-maching and hand-sewing techniques before beginning to specialize in millinery. (This text does not thoroughly cover basic sewing skills, as there are many good sources that teach them.) Other skills that aid milliners include basic pattern-making knowledge, a good understanding of fabrics, and excellent problem-solving and organizational skills.

To become a good milliner, one needs to know more than techniques and basic methods. Millinery requires a certain sensitivity, a feel for the aesthetics of fine hatmaking. A really good milliner has a light touch—and his or her hats, though strong and able to take the abuse of being used, have a delicate "lightly-kissed-together-by-angels" look. A really good milliner's work is meticulous, with extra attention paid to every lovely detail, from the initial pattern making through the final decoration.

Millinery, like tailoring, is not for everybody, and not everyone has the special delicate touch that's necessary to be a *great* milliner. Anyone can make a hat—it is this touch that separates a true milliner/artist from a mere hatmaker.

This book covers how to get started, basic stitches, basic pattern making (which is where excellent three-dimensional reasoning skills come in handy), and other basic tools and techniques, taking students through the construction of several basic hats from a range of standard hatmaking materials. Throughout, I try to address the aesthetics that are desirable in a good milliner. Hopefully, the successful student will learn to, as I like to say, "Craft with a capital C, not Kraft with a klunky K."

1
Before You Begin

Before you begin making a hat—even before you make a pattern—it's important to consider organization, your workspace, and the tools and materials a milliner needs. This chapter discusses all of these, and—since milliners and theatrical costumers often work with hazardous chemicals—also includes some notes about safety.

Organization and Workspace

A most important skill for a milliner is organization. You should not only organize your work area and tools, but also your paperwork. By making charts of everything you have to accomplish, you will be able to easily recognize and prioritize your projects, working time, and work schedule. Keep track of the actors' fitting schedules so that you can fit your hats on them as soon as possible before you finish the hats.

Before you make any patterns or begin constructing hats, make a large chart that lists all of the actors' names and their head measurements, like the one in Figure 1.1. List the character each actor plays and all the hats each character wears. Sometimes an actor plays more than one character and often a character has more than one hat— use as many lines on your chart as you need to accommodate this information. Include on the chart a place to indicate if the hat is going to be built, pulled from stock and altered, or purchased. Include space to list the fabrics and trims to be used for each hat. Make a place to indicate if the hat has been fit on the actor and if any additional work needs to be done. Leave space to check off when each hat is done. Include space to make miscellaneous notes about each hat.

Show Title: _____ Date: _____

Actor Name	Character	Head Size	Hairline	Front-to-Back	Side-to-Side	Other	Description of Hat	Pull/Buy/Build	Work Notes

Figure 1.1 Chart for keeping track of a production's hats and actors.

Date all of your paperwork. It is amazing how quickly your lists can change throughout the construction process. If there are any casting changes in the play, it can be very important to know when in the process you made a list or a chart. If you make your lists on a computer, set up a template so that the date is automatically updated using a date-and-time field.

An organized workspace will make a huge difference in your overall productivity. Take the trouble and time to clean up your workspace at the end of each day—especially if there is more than one person working in your area, which is usually the case. Being able to work quickly and efficiently is essential to the quick-paced production schedule of most theater companies. Keeping your tools and materials in their proper places will actually increase the time you have to work on projects, since you won't have to spend time searching for them.

Keep your workspace orderly as you work. Keep a large trash can next to the workspace and a small trash can right next to you so that trash and remnants don't pile up. If you don't have the luxury of a custodial service cleaning up after you, sweep around and under your work area at the end of each day. Make cleaning up fun for yourself and your fellow crafters. For the last fifteen minutes of every workday, I like to have everyone stop work and together clean up the shop and put away tools and materials. If you make a fun ritual out of cleanup (and even include fun music), you'll help relieve the day's tensions and keep up morale and productivity—your own as well as everyone else's.

I cannot stress enough the importance of good lighting. I speak from personal experience—a poorly lit workspace causes eyestrain and fatigue, and can even be dangerous while using a sewing machine, needles, scissors, and other sharp tools. Buy your own swing-arm lamp with a high-watt bulb if you have to. You can always take it with you wherever you go to work. Be wary of fluorescent lights. They alter the appearance of colors, often making them very different from how they will look under stage lights. Fluorescent lights cause fading damage to fabrics. Avoid giving yourself a headache: Make sure you have good light so you can see small details easily. Remember, a good milliner wants to pay close attention to the smallest detail—but you don't want to ruin your eyesight to do it.

To help stay organized, invest in your own toolbox—I would suggest one with a lock. Many milliners I know make a canvas tool caddy that they pin up on the wall. A caddy has pockets for each tool, and the whole thing rolls up neatly for travel and storage. Put your name on your tools. The cost of tools quickly adds up. Protect

Show
Character
Actor
Hat Type
Trim/Fabric
Note

Figure 1.2 Materials for a hat tag

your investment and prevent confusion by engraving your name on all scissors, pliers, and other metal tools, and use a permanent marker to identify rulers and other nonmetal tools.

As you start working on the hats for a play, you'll quickly accumulate a pile of fabrics, trims, patterns, and hats. When I first acquire materials for hat making, I quickly staple or tape a label to them. I make and use preprinted tags with places to identify the show, character, actor, hat type, trim and fabric, and any other information I feel is important (Figure 1.2). It's a good idea to make and print out your own tags before you begin to work, while you are setting up the workspace. I keep a stack of them in a small shoe box with my millinery supplies.

Tools and Supplies

Having the right tools and supplies will make your life as a milliner easier and happier. You will need certain tools to work on the projects in this book and on other hats. Many of them can be found in costume shops, but some may be more difficult to get. A well-stocked millinery shop should have them all—and then some. The list that follows is fairly thorough, but is by no means complete. It is not in any particular order of importance. I hope you will always look for new tools and materials that will make your work easier and more efficient. Any fabulous time-savers you use will help you make a more professional-looking product. Figure 1.3 shows some of the basic hand tools and sewing supplies you'll need.

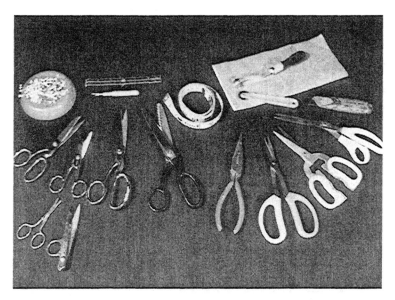

Figure 1.3 Basic hand tools and sewing supplies for hatmaking.

Scissors

The first thing you need is a good pair of sharp dressmaking shears (scissors). These should be used *for fabric only—nothing else*. Most milliners have several different kinds and sizes of scissors. Designate one pair for fabric, one pair for paper and cardboard, and maybe even one pair for buckram. I like to keep a good pair of sharp, expensive scissors for fabric and cheap "disposable" scissors for tough nonfabric materials. Pinking shears can come in handy—they put a zigzag edge on fabric that deters fraying. I have recently added a small pair of tin snips and a small pair of gardener's pruning shears to my tool collection. You might also want some small delicate scissors, like embroidery shears, tailor's points, and small personal-grooming scissors (found in the fingernail care section of your local drugstore). It is important to eventually have a range of sizes and types that will suit a broad range of purposes. It is also important that your really expensive scissors get used only by you—different hands will stress the blades in different places, so the more people that use them, the greater the wear and tear on them.

Pliers

You will need several kinds of pliers. Two good pairs of needle-nose pliers will come in very handy. Make sure that you have at least one good pair of sharp wire cutters. If you do a lot of millinery work, these might need to be replaced frequently. Lots of needle-nose pliers have a built-in wire cutter, but I recommend you have a separate wire cutter; that way you can hold items with the needle-nose pliers and cut with the cutting pliers. I have four pairs of needle-nose pliers—two with teeth on the prongs and two with smooth prongs. Sometimes you don't want teeth to leave marks on the materials. A good toolbox will include at least one pair of channel-lock pliers and at least one pair of regular pliers. You won't use these often, but when you need them, even if it's just to open a stubborn can of hat sizing, it's nice to have them.

Thread

You will need heavy-duty and regular-duty thread. In rare instances, you might need prewaxed thread. (I recommend that you not use prewaxed or waxed thread. It goes through fabrics smoothly, but it doesn't stay knotted well. Any wardrobe supervisor will tell you that things sewn with waxed thread tend to come undone with wear.) Other kinds of string and filament that can be useful to have around but that aren't used for the projects in this book are kite string, fishing line, "invisible" thread, elastic thread, and metallic threads. I have recently started using fusible thread. It looks like clear plastic thread, but after it is stitched into fabric you can use an iron to melt it and it becomes a thin line of glue.

Sewing Supplies

You will need various other typical sewing supplies, including upholstery needles (be sure to get a good curved needle), thimbles, and tape measures. Try to get a small curved needle from a surgical supplier. These are smaller and more delicate than curved upholstery needles. You will need hand-sewing needles in a variety of sizes and lengths. I like to get size 10 milliner's needles because they are long, thin, and strong. You will need good straight pins. There are many kinds of straight pins, and you may eventually develop a preference. I recommend starting with long quilting pins, which are sharp and have a plastic ball on one end, making them easy to use—especially if you don't have long fingernails. A magnetic pin holder keeps pins from ending up on the floor. Get a seam ripper—and since they are cheap, replace it often to ensure that you always have a sharp one. Get a patterning tracing wheel and trac-ing transfer marking papers to use with them. Supplies that you don't need for the projects in this book but that you should eventually obtain include interfacings of various weights, fusible interfacings, fusible transfer web, cord elastic, $\frac{1}{2}$-inch elas-tic, 1-inch elastic, a clear quilting ruler marked in a grid pattern, and seam gauges. Always be on the lookout for new sewing supplies and try new products when you discover them. Never be afraid to try new tools and techniques.

Craft Supplies

Craft supplies you will need include brown craft paper, poster board or card-stock paper, cellophane tape, masking tape, rubber gloves, and long stainless steel push-pins. Look for very thin all-purpose metal wire or beading wire, which is available on small spools or cards. It is often available in department stores in the craft sec-tion. Since it is inexpensive, collect a variety of gauges and colors (silver, gold, pewter). Measuring tools and straightedges you will need include rulers of various lengths, an assortment of French curves, and a couple of drafting triangles (Figure 1.4). You will also need a few butane lighters.

Figure 1.4 Measuring tools.

Specialty Millinery Supplies

You will need head blocks in various sizes (Figure 1.5). These are specially made wooden shapes that come in $1/2$-inch increments. If you can't afford them, you might try making your own—but since I am not a woodworking expert, I won't tell you how to do it. I have heard of people carving chunks of Styrofoam into head blocks, but I am not sure how well such a thing would hold up over long-term use.

You will also need buckram, a thick, loosely woven fabric that is infused with a sturdy water-soluble sizing. You will need a good-quality millinery felt to make felt hoods or cartwheels, and millinery wire to make wire hats. Millinery wire is covered with thread and comes in different gauges—the lower the gauge number, the thicker the wire. I recommend getting one roll each of thick, medium, and thin to start. I like to use No. 19 wire, and that is the gauge I use in this book. You will need hat sizing (Figure 1.6) and hat-sizing thinner, which are available from millinery supply companies. You will also need $1/2$-inch-wide nylon "horsehair" braid. Get it in clear if you can—you will be able to paint it any color you like, but left clear it will disappear into the wearer's hair.

Major Equipment

One of the larger items you will need is a sewing machine that does a variable-length straight stitch and a variable-width zigzag stitch. A powerful, sturdy machine that

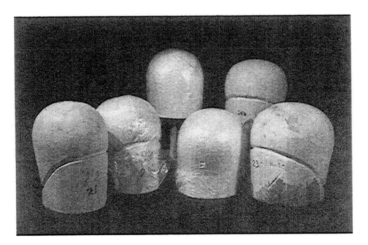

Figure 1.5 Wooden head blocks.

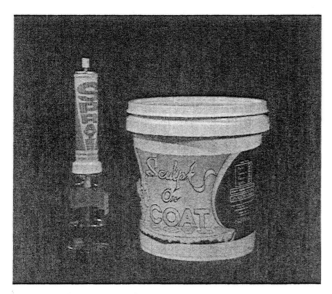

Figure 1.6 Hat sizing in a Preval sprayer and a bucket of
Sculpt Or Coat.

does a few stitches is much more desirable than a delicate electronic one that does
thousands of stitches. Get a machine that accepts different presser feet, and in addition to the standard foot, have an assortment of specialty presser feet—at least have
a zigzag foot, a rolled-hem foot, and a ruffle-making foot. A portable tabletop machine that has a free arm is nice to have, especially when you are stitching around a
huge hat brim. It is easier if you aren't trying to fight the machine's table or cabinet
while you work. Remember to replace your machine needles often and be sure to
use the appropriate needle for the material you are using.

You should also have an edge-overlock sewing machine (a serger). You can do
millinery work without one, but it will make fast work of finishing fabric edges.
Have an assortment of colors of serger thread, and be sure you don't use serger
thread to do machine sewing or hand sewing. Replace the needles and cutting tool
on the serger as part of regular maintenance—dull blades and needles result in poor-
quality work.

You will need a steamer—a tabletop one works best. The Jiffy Steamer Company
makes one specifically for millinery work. Get an iron, an ironing board, and an assortment of pressing tools, hams, and a sleeve board. I occasionally need a pressing

needle-board to work with pile fabrics such as velvet. You will also need at least one large pot and access to hot water.

Chemicals

You will need a number of chemicals, including millinery glue (also called bridal glue), contact cement (go to a shoe-repair store to get a really strong one), spray adhesive, acetone, denatured alcohol, and spray paint. As mentioned earlier, you'll also need millinery sizing (also called lacquer) and lacquer thinner. See the "Safety Notes" section of this chapter for important information about working with these chemicals.

Miscellaneous

Miscellaneous tools and materials you will sometimes need include aluminum foil, plastic wrap, a hammer, disposable paintbrushes, sandpaper, pressing cloths and spray starch or sizing, a compass to make circles, a matte knife and blades, floral tape and floral wire, cotton batting or stuffing, a hair dryer, plastic hair combs in clear and tortoiseshell, forced-air disposable spray bottles from the hardware store, assorted snaps, hook-and-loop fastening tape, muslin or other mock-up fabrics, and various fabrics to use to cover hats. You will need grosgrain ribbon and French belting (look for natural fiber content). Good grosgrain ribbon can easily be ironed into a lovely curve and comes in a variety of colors. Black, white, and beige are the most useful—you can always dye white ribbon to match any color of fabric. Buy this from a reputable millinery supply company—cheap grosgrain does not iron into a curve and is not very useful in millinery.

Spray Paint Nozzle

When you need to spray paint, look in the paint aisle at a hardware or department store for detachable trigger sprayers (Figure 1.7). These simple and cheap handles snap onto the top of most paint cans and keep the paint farther away from your hands, which is cleaner. If you are doing a lot of spraying, they will dramatically decrease your hand fatigue. They also give you better control over the paint application, creating a smoother, more even coating.

Glue Guns

Many people who work with crafts love to use a hot-melt or cool-melt glue gun. I too love my glue gun and use it for many things—but rarely do I use it for millinery.

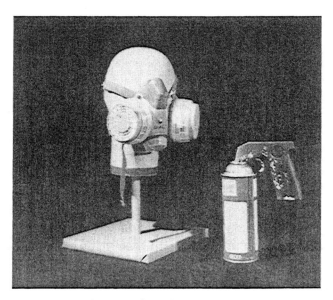

Figure 1.7 Respirator (left) and spray paint can with detachable trigger.

Hot- or cold-melt glue soaks into fabrics—and hats are mostly fabric. This means that any hat made or decorated with a glue gun is virtually unalterable. It is highly useful to have in your stock only hats that can be altered. Who would want a stock full of hats that can't be used again? The only time I use hot-melt glue to make a hat is when I know the hat will never be able to be turned into something else. For example, I used hot-melt glue to construct hats for the chorus of ladies in the beauty shop scene in the musical *Grease!* I knew that these hair-roller-covered bonnets would never be able to be made into anything else.

Safety Notes

Milliners often work with dangerous and hazardous chemicals. All chemical products that are sold in the United States, from spray paint and millinery glue to millinery sizing and denatured alcohol, have documentation about their toxicity and other useful information about their characteristics. These are called material safety data sheets (MSDS). These sheets, though often pretty technical, are full of useful information. I recommend that you get them for any unfamiliar products you are going to use. At the Utah Shakespearean Festival, the MSDS are kept in special notebooks in every workspace, and are always available for any person working there. MSDS will provide you with information about the health consequences of using these chemicals and any precautions you should take. MSDS are available from retailers who sell the products, and some are available online.

When using any chemical, read the label to see if there are any health precautions recommended. I have found that the biggest problem in workspace safety is usually not a lack of safety equipment, but rather the fact that people just don't use it all the time. In the costume craft business, you may not be exposed to chemicals for long sustained periods of time, but multiple little exposures over time add up. There is not a costume item in the world that is more important than your health. You must act now to protect your health down the road.

If you have a spray booth, use it to draw fumes away from you as you work. If you don't have a spray booth, work outside with toxic products. I always use a respirator (see Figure 1.7), a half-mask one that filters out organic vapors, paint particles, and dust. Filters are available that will protect you from all kinds of things, from dust to radiation. Basically you want as little between your lungs and the air as possible, so that your lungs don't have to work any harder than necessary. A word of caution: It is not legal for students to use respirators on some university or college campuses. Some individuals are unaware that they have hidden respiratory problems that could be triggered by using a respirator. If you use a respirator, make sure to first get tested for such problems. If you have not been tested and cleared to use a respirator, don't use it—especially if you are working alone. Check with your school or employer for their safety equipment policies and procedures before investing in a respirator. For more information and ideas about respirators, see exercise 3 at the end of this chapter.

Wear eye protection when working with anything that could create airborne particles, including anything that is sprayed; when working with or cutting wire; and when drilling or cutting any material. Use rubber gloves to keep paint off your skin. When working with solvents like denatured alcohol, be extra careful and be sure to wear rubber gloves that are impervious to organic solvents—rubber gloves from the grocery store won't give you enough protection. You can get appropriate gloves from a lab supply catalog. Never allow organic solvents to come into contact with bare skin, and never breathe their fumes. Check the contents of any glues you use for hidden solvents—many contain acetone.

Make sure there is an adequately stocked first-aid kit in your work area, and that the items in it haven't expired. Make sure there is a properly charged fire extinguisher nearby. Post emergency phone numbers next to every phone, especially if 911 service isn't available in your area. Include poison control center numbers. If you work around costume shops regularly, it is a good idea to take a first-aid course and CPR training.

As part of your first-aid preparedness, check to see if your state has "Good Samaritan" laws. These laws protect you from legal action after the fact when you have offered help to an accident victim. Know the legal ramifications of helping others.

If you ever feel unsure or unsafe about what you are doing or what you are being asked to do, DON'T DO IT. If you are unsure about a project or machine or tool, ask your supervisor or teacher. See if there is a different or safer solution to your problem. Always think through a process prior to beginning any potentially dangerous task. It is important to remember that your body and your health and safety are very important, and without them, you will not be able to make hats.

Exercises

1. Put together your own MSDS notebook for all of the chemicals in your costume shop, paying special attention to the products you will be using in millinery. Divide them by types of products: glues, paint, etc. Highlight the most useful information on each sheet.

2. Make and post a chart of emergency phone numbers in your area, including fire, ambulance, and poison control centers. What other emergency services should you include?

3. If your workplace or school permits it, arrange to have a respirator test to find out if it is safe for you to use a respirator. Check with your university's health services to see if they offer or can recommend a source for the tests. See if you can get a lung test and a test for the fit of the mask on the face (if you can smell anything through the mask, you have a loose, potentially dangerous fit).

4. Have a first-aid specialist talk to the class about basic first-aid techniques, especially about how to deal with materials in the eyes, cuts, burns, and chem-

ical spills and poisoning. Ask the specialist to talk about appropriate safety procedures around spilled bodily fluids. You might even try to get a first-aid certificate if you have the money and time.

5. Have a fire specialist talk to the class about how to use a fire extinguisher and other fire safety issues, such as how to use a fire blanket. Does your shop or school have a fire evacuation plan? Are there smoke detectors in place? Are they functioning properly?

2
Planning

You start making a hat by planning, which involves getting the correct measurements, considering the hat's scale and design, and choosing the hat's fabric and other materials. Let's take a look at the parts of a hat, then go through the planning steps.

The Parts of a Hat

Hats are made up of a few basic parts (Figure 2.1). The crown is the part that covers the head. It may be a single piece or two pieces, called a sideband and a tip. A top hat has a sideband and a tip, and a cowboy hat has a one-piece crown. The brim is the visor extension on a crown. It may encircle the crown (like on a Royal Canadian Mounted Policeman's hat), or it may extend from just part of the crown (like on a baseball cap). Some hats are only a crown with no brim, and some hats are all brim with no crown, allowing the hair to show in the middle. Some hats, like a Gothic peaked cap (a Robin Hood hat), have a brim that is an extension of the crown that is simply folded up. Some hats, like a Tudor gabled headdress, have neither crown nor brim, but are their own unique structures.

The inside of a hat should be lined. Linings prevent the inner seams and rough edges from getting tangled with the wearer's hair. A headsize ribbon is often stitched around the bottom inside edge of a hat to prevent the hat from stretching larger. A small ribbon bow or tag should mark the center back of the hat, making it easier for the wearer to find.

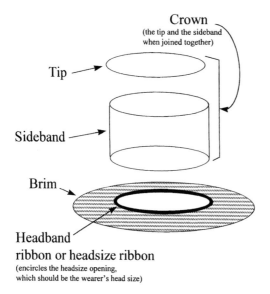

Crown
(the tip and the sideband
when joined together)

Tip

Sideband

Brim

Headband
ribbon or headsize ribbon
(encircles the headsize opening,
which should be the wearer's head size)

Not shown:
  ° lining inside the crown
  ° ribbon or bow marking the center back

Figure 2.1 The parts of a hat.

Measuring

Most working milliners have their own favorite ways of measuring, and some are quite comfortable working with industry-standard hat sizes. The industry-standard hat-size chart in Figure 2.2 shows the correspondence between head size, in both inches and centimeters, and standard hat size. If you are working with other costume crafters, it might be easiest to keep track of all measurements in inches—it will save you time and energy if you do not have to translate numbers as you work. One student I had who was from Poland preferred keeping track of measurements in centimeters, and all of her personal tools were marked in centimeters. Whatever your preferred unit of measure, the most important thing is to be precise and to take all of your head measurement the same way. Make sure all people involved in the project—your assistant, a fellow milliner, others in the costume shop—remain consis-

Head Size		Standard
Inches	Centimeters	Hat Size
18¾	48	6
19⅛	49	6⅛
19½	50	6¼
19⅞	51	6⅜
20¼	52	6½
20¾	53	6⅝
21⅛	54	6¾
21½	55	6⅞
21⅞	56	7
22¼	57	7⅛
22⅝	58	7¼
23	59	7⅜
23¼	60	7½
23⅞	61	7⅝
24¼	62	7¾
24⅝	63	7⅞
25	64	8

Figure 2.2 Industry-standard hat-size chart.

tent with how measurements are taken and recorded. Clear communications and consistency will make the costume construction process more pleasant and efficient.

Whether you are using inches or centimeters, be precise down to the closest fraction. If your exact measurement is not listed on the hat-size chart, round up to the next size. It is always easier to fix a slightly larger hat than to try to make a small hat larger. I recommend that you keep a framed copy of the conversion chart posted on the wall in your millinery work area for easy reference.

It is very important for a milliner to take all of his or her own measurements whenever possible. I once had a draper take head measurements for me, and the results were skewed when she added *ease*, a common practice in pattern making that allows a little extra room in the finished garment for ease of movement. It was simply her normal way to take measurements, and she didn't realize the problems it created for me. Unlike the body, the top of the human head does not breathe, flex, or change shape radically, and no ease is needed—in fact, added ease simply gives you less accurate information from which to work. Your hats must fit well so they will stay on the wearer's head.

The most important measurement you need is the head size. This is the measurement around the head, just above the ears and eyebrows and around the largest part of the back of the head, where a hat typically sits (Figure 2.3). Be sure you do not take this measurement around a large hairstyle, a bun, or a ponytail. If necessary, ask the actor to take down his or her hair so you can get an accurate measurement.

The hairline measurement starts at the center top of the forehead where most people's hairline starts, goes at an angle across the ears and down around and below the fullest part of the back of the head, and finishes at the base of the skull where the neck and head meet (Figure 2.4). If the actor is bald or balding, take the measurement from where the hair would typically start, a few inches above the eyebrows.

Two other useful measurements are the front-to-back measurement and the side-to-side measurement. Both are based on the placement of the head-size measurement. The front-to-back measurement begins at the forehead and goes over the top of the head to the back, beginning and ending where the head-size measurement was taken. The side-to-side measurement goes across the head from above one ear to above the other ear, again beginning and ending at the head-size measurement.

As you take measurements, make note of anything you might need to remember as you make the hat. If the actor is bald or balding, note it on your measurement sheet—you may wish to include extra padding to compensate for the lack of hair, which usually acts as a built-in head protector. I even include a little sketch of the actor's hairline if it is unusual so that I can remember. Include such information as particularly thick or particularly long hair (which might end up being tucked under a hat to hide it). Note if the actor has an unusually shaped head, such as a very high or protruding forehead or exceptionally large ears, or a very small or large head.

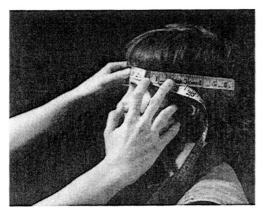
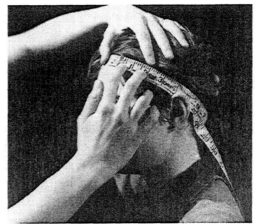

Figure 2.3   Measuring head size.

Figure 2.4 Measuring the hairline.

Get copies of actors' headshots if you can so you can not only remember their hairlines, but can also pattern your hats with the shape of a particular actor's face in mind. I like to tape headshots up around my workspace for quick and easy reference.

Before making any patterns, check with the costume designer and the wig and makeup designers to see which actors will be wearing wigs. Sometimes it is beneficial to measure an actor's head with a styled wig on it. When working with wigged actors, you will probably make an educated guess about the final head size. It is best to find out early if the wigs will be thick or thin, and if the styling will add considerably to the head-size measurement. I usually add from ¾ to 1-¼ inches to the head size when I know a wig will be under the hat I am making.

Considering Scale and Design

When you work as a milliner in the theater, you typically work with a costume designer whose designs or renderings may or may not be clear and easy to understand. Before you begin making the hats for a show, make an appointment with the designer to go over each costume rendering specifically looking at hats. Have a pencil and paper and write down everything you learn about each hat. Ask about anything that is unclear. What does the hat look like from the back? What, if anything, does the hat have to do onstage? (I once made a Victorian lady's hat that got thrown off the stage like a Frisbee!) Is the hat worn the whole time it is onstage, or is it removed from or put onto the actor onstage? How does the hat affix to the head? Are hat pins involved? Do you need to provide hairpin loops? Does the costume rendering show scale accurately? Use the face in the sketch as a guide to determine scale, and check your findings with the designer. Some designers are very good at depicting the scale they intend, but not all are. Find out what fabrics and trimmings the designer intends for each hat. If the design of the hat is based on historical research, ask for your own copy of the research and examine it thoroughly. It is amazing how much better you can understand what you are being asked to make when you look at the same material that inspired the designer. It is never out of line to ask for more information, more research, or more sketches to clarify the process for yourself. And remember, a good designer wants the finished hat to be as fabulous as you want it to be, and will usually be glad to provide additional clarifying materials. The more complete your information at the beginning, the fewer surprises you'll have after construction begins.

Choosing Materials

When choosing the materials to make a hat, do your research. You can often find documentation that tells you what materials were commonly used to make a particular type of hat, or the process used. Many costume technologists don't realize how much better they can become by doing research. When working with historical millinery sources, remember that some materials, such as willow, are not available anymore. Other materials, though available, might not be suitable for stage costumes, which often need to be made sturdier than the original garments were. Ask yourself, "For whom was this material written?" Often, millinery books were intended for personal at-home sewing. Remember, you are not making a museum-piece replica: You are creating a hat that is sturdy and very useable.

Decide whether your hat needs a support structure. Buckram is usually used for the understructure of stiff hats. Sometimes you may need to make a stiff buckram base and then cover it with fabric or padding, or even wrap it loosely with fabric to create the illusion of a soft hat. A hat that is extremely stiff or that needs to be extremely strong should be made of crown-weight buckram, a two-layered buckram. If you don't have crown-weight buckram, you can make you own by gluing two layers together.

Some soft hats don't need stiffened understructures. Generally, use fabric for soft caps and draped hats. Usually, a costume designer will be choosing fabrics for you, but you might have to add stiffness with interfacing, which is available in various weights. If the fabric you have been given to work with is too stiff, try washing it to soften it. Just be careful not to shrink the fabric.

I talk about wire, felt, and straw hats later in the book. Keep in mind that some hats combine hard and soft structures, the basic shape being made of stiff buckram, with fabric covering it or draped around it.

Exercises

1. Research and find at least five different wigs styled in various hairstyles. If necessary, style your own as best you can, or seek others' help. Try to include period hairstyles that you might encounter when working on plays, such as a large Gibson girl hairstyle or a short-cropped page boy. Place each wig on heads of various sizes and take measurements over the wigs. (Use fellow classmates, or actors who are not busy.) Note the differences on a chart, being sure to include each actor's true head-size, side-to-side, front-to-back, and hairline measurements. Note the wig's style and characteristics, and the measurements taken over the wigs. Do you find any consistency or predictability in the amount that wigs add to measurements?

2. Measure five people's heads in both inches and centimeters. Note the measurements on a chart. Be sure to list the standard hat size for each person's head.

3. Make a list of questions to ask a costume designer before beginning to make the hats she has designed. If possible, interview an experienced costume designer and go over some of the sketches from a show that has already been produced. Pretend you are going to be the milliner for the show and ask the designer your list of questions. When you are done, ask the designer to give you pointers on what you should have asked but didn't. If possible, examine

some of the hats that were used in the show and discuss with the designer why things were done as they were. Amend your list of questions to include things that you didn't ask but should have.

4. Find ten pictures of hats from one historical period. You might choose the early Italian Renaissance, or the mid-1800s. Make a list of the characteristics of the hats you have chosen. What materials were used to make them? What are they trimmed and decorated with? How are the hats kept on the wearer's head? Can you determine the basic shape of the hat? Is it a soft cap or is it a hard construction? Can you find basic hat shapes in hat catalogs that could be turned into the hats in your research? (A quick Internet search for "hat catalogs" should result in several sources for basic hat forms.)

5. Using the same ten pictures, think about the following. Hats are worn for many reasons: to indicate social standing or wealth, for religious reasons, to create sex appeal, for particular jobs (a nurse's cap), for practical function such as keeping the wearer warm. Hats tell the viewer a lot about the wearer—whether that information is true or not is another matter. Sometimes a person wears a hat to try to make a statement. What do the hats in your pictures tell you about the wearer? Sometimes you can find hints about the "language" of hats in your research. What are some modern hat trends, and what statement does a hat seem to convey?

6. Find a picture of a hat from the Gothic period of Europe and bring it to class. Be sure no one else sees your picture. Make a drawing that shows the hat on a person's head, just as a costume designer might draw it. Now exchange drawings with one of your classmates. Interview each other about the hat using the list of questions you created in question 3. After you think you understand the drawing you were given, look over the research on which it was based. Add any other questions you should have asked to your list.

3
Basic Pattern Knowledge

This chapter discusses the basics of creating and working with hat patterns.

Working with Patterns

Any costume pattern maker will tell you: When making any pattern, even if it is only one piece, label all the pieces. Include the name of the hat part (for example, "brim"). Name each hat (for example, "Large Blue Pillbox"), and include the name on every pattern piece to make sure you can keep all your patterns sorted out. I like to include wearer information as well—the actor's name and character. Include the play title, act, and scene if that helps you identify the hat.

I keep each pattern stored in its own manila envelope. On the envelope I list the play's title and all of the information I put on the pattern itself. I also like to put a line drawing of the hat on the outside of the envelope, and note the play's time period.

When a show is over, I save the patterns that worked well and discard those that didn't. I like to file away my patterns for possible future use. You might organize patterns by time period (my favorite method) or by type of hat. Once you have a collection of patterns, you might be surprised at how often you use them. It is a wonderful time-saver if you don't have to "reinvent the wheel" when you start a new show. Some milliners are stingy with their patterns, like a chef guarding recipes, but I like to share mine, and I have even exchanged patterns with other milliners, which increased all of our collections.

Pattern Marks

Mark your pattern with standard pattern markings, the most common of which are shown here. Be sure to provide notches—marks on the edges—to show how the pieces are supposed to line up.

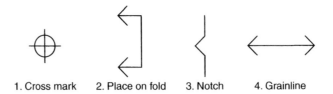

1. Cross mark   2. Place on fold   3. Notch   4. Grainline

1. The cross mark is a way to perfectly match two or more layers of fabric. Use it to indicate where a spot on one layer of fabric should line up with a spot on another layer.

2. The joined double arrow means "place this edge of the pattern on the fold of a piece of fabric." Use this mark when a piece needs to be cut symmetrically.

3. Notches show where to line up the edges of cut-out pieces of fabric before sewing them together. Usually a single notch indicates "front" and two notches next to each other indicate "back."

4. The grainline mark shows the direction of the fabric's *grain*—the longest threads in a piece of woven fabric, which run parallel to the selvage edge. Placed at a diagonal to the grain, this mark shows that the fabric is to be cut on the bias.

Deciding Where to Begin

Creating a pattern for a costume piece can be a long, involved exploration, but you probably won't have much time to find the absolute best solution to every pattern-making problem. Even now, after years of making hats, I often wish I had more time to spend developing and perfecting a pattern. Remember to work quickly. If a pattern just isn't going well, or if it's extremely frustrating and difficult, you may be trying to make the hat more difficult than it should be. Often the simple solution is the best solution.

A good tip for beginning milliners is to use existing patterns. You can find hat patterns in commercial pattern books and millinery books. The more you work with pattern shapes and the more familiar they become, the easier it will become to make patterns from scratch.

Before you start making patterns, remember that the human head is longer from the front to the back than it is wide from side to side: It is an oval, not a circle. Later, I cover the basic oval pattern in more detail.

Other than using existing patterns, how do you begin to make a pattern for a hat? This is not an easy question to answer. Many milliners approach their patterns almost intuitively, relying on their three-dimensional logic skills to "see" a hat's shapes. If you can look at a flattened box and see in your mind how the put-together box would look, you are a person with good three-dimensional logic. Three-dimensional logic works backwards, too—if you have it, you can look at a finished shape and tell how it would look flattened out. A milliner who has this ability can just look at a shape and know how to pattern it. But there are other ways to approach pattern making.

One way is to break the hat down into basic geometric shapes. Look for the fundamental geometry in a hat as a way to start making it. Perhaps your hat is a half-sphere sitting on top of a cylinder. You can begin the pattern by making a cylinder shape and then shaping paper over a head block or other object to get the half-sphere to put on top of it. I have seen milliners use salad bowls to drape rounded shapes—always look for useful shapes in extraordinary places.

Another way to get a pattern is to take a rubbing from an existing hat. Put paper up against the hat and mark and cut the paper until you have copied the shape exactly. This is not as easy as it sounds, but sometimes it is easier than starting from thin air. When you do this, lay out the pattern rubbing and correct any irregularities with a ruler or French curve. Be sure to add seam allowances where necessary.

As you make a pattern and then a mock-up, work with a head block with a head size the same as or slightly larger than your actor's head so that you can keep checking it as you go. Remember, it is easier to make a pattern slightly smaller than it is to enlarge it. Since the head block is wooden, you can even pin the pattern pieces into it. If you are using card stock, you can tape the pieces together. If you are using fabric, you can pin or baste them together.

The really hard part when making a pattern is taping the pieces together accurately without leaving gaps between them. I find that it is easier if I put tape all along one edge of a pattern piece and then attach it to the other pieces. Then I don't have to keep tearing new pieces of tape while I am trying to hold the pattern pieces in the correct place.

I also rely on my pattern collection when I am making a hat. It has been very helpful to keep a collection of basic hat shapes as I invent them. Every time you make or come across a basic hat shape or a slight variation of a shape, be sure to save that pattern. Often you can copy a basic shape, then slightly alter it to get the shape you want. For example, if you had to make a pillbox shape whose top was severely tilted from the front to the back, you might start by making a basic pillbox hat pattern, then *splitting and spreading* it to get the correct shape. Splitting and spreading is a method of adding to a pattern's dimensions by physically cutting the pattern, moving the pieces apart, filling in the spaces with scrap paper and taping it together into its new expanded shape.

Mock-ups

Once you have created it, make a mock-up of the hat to try on the actor's head (Figure 3.1). Use materials that simulate the actual fabrics you'll use on the finished hat. Card stock and muslin work well to simulate buckram and almost any fabric.

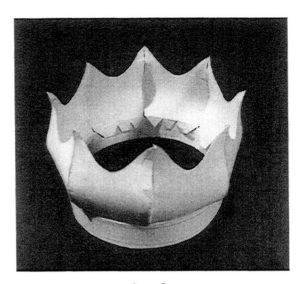

Figure 3.1 Pattern mock-up for a crown.

Don't worry about making the mock-up too detailed. A mock-up's primary purpose is to let you discover the pattern, size, and scale and shape of the hat. Decorative details like large feathers can be held up to the mock-up when it is on the actor's head to show the designer how the finished hat will appear. The mock-up should give the designer a good sense of the finished hat. If your mock-up has missed the mark, which sometimes happens, it may be necessary to begin the process again and make a new pattern and a new mock-up. If there are only slight changes needed, indicate them on the mock-up with a marker or pins. Be sure to write down detailed descriptions of what changes need to be made. I usually make these notes right on the mock-up itself. Back at your workspace, correct the pattern before making the hat.

Try to have a mock-up of each hat done for the first costume fitting with each actor. If you are ready to fit a hat on an actor, check with the designer or costume shop manager to see if you can arrange a fitting, or if they will add a few minutes to the costume fitting for a hat fitting. It is important to fit your mock-ups on actors as soon as possible so that you'll have enough time to fix problems and make the finished hat. In some theaters, you can arrange special fittings with actors to work out problems that don't require anyone but the milliner to be present.

The Basic Cone Shape

One of the most common hat shapes you will use is the basic cone shape. This is a more difficult pattern, though, and you may want to work your way through the basic pillbox shapes before attempting it. To make a cone, first draw a circle, being sure to mark the center point of the circle. Then use a straightedge to draw a line from the center point to the outer edge of the circle. Cut out the circle with scissors, then cut the on the straight line to the center point. Overlap the two straight edges of the circle and slide them over each other until you have the cone shape you desire. Many hats that are based on the cone shape use a section of the basic cone with the pointed end cut off and a flat tip inserted. This cut-off shape is known by various names: the truncated cone, the fez, the truncated hennin. The tricky part in making a cone-shaped hat is to keep in mind that the human head is oval, not round. Depending on exactly how the hat fits, you may or may not want to use a round tip—you may want to use an oval tip.

Another way to achieve a basic truncated cone shape is to begin with a basic pillbox pattern, then at regular intervals split and spread the sideband at right angles along the bottom of the head-size opening. The more space you add into the splits, the more severe the angle of the sideband you will get.

I constantly remind beginning milliners that millinery is not an exact science, but an art; it requires artistic intuition, imagination, and inspiration. Often, a less-than-precise method works beautifully. Here is a quick, less accurate way of making a tip for your hat: If you have patterned the sideband and need to pattern a tip to put into it, begin by measuring around the top of the sideband and put two marks indicating the center front and center back (you can fold the sideband into exact halves to find the center front and center back). On a separate piece of paper, draw a straight line down the center of a piece of card stock. Turn the sideband upside down and line up the center front and center back marks on the line. Tape the hat down to ensure it doesn't move and make sure that it is roughly shaped in an oval, then trace around the opening. Remove the sideband and use a French curve to correct half of the tip pattern. Double-check the measurement around the corrected half of the tip—it should be the same as half the distance around the top of the sideband. Erase and adjust if necessary. When it is the correct measurement, cut out that half of the tip pattern. Fold this half over the half that isn't cut out and trace it onto that half. Cut out the second half of the pattern, unfold, and you have a tip pattern.

Basic Oval Pattern

Many milliners begin patterning with a basic oval shape the same size as, or slightly larger than, the hat they are making, and then add a sideband and brim. A 23-inch head size might mean you would start with a 23½-inch basic oval pattern. The extra ½ inch will allow for fabric covering on the inside. I have made a basic head oval pattern in heavy card stock for every size on my hat-size conversion chart. Each one is clearly labeled and having them saves me a great deal of time whenever I make a hat.

To make an oval pattern from scratch, begin by drawing a straight line down the center of a piece of paper. Intersect that line at a right angle, making a cross in the center of the page. Use a compass to make a circle using the center of the cross as the center of the circle. Set the compass at 3⅜ inches so the circle ends up being 6¾ inches across and up and down on the lines that cross inside it. Cut out the circle, then cut it in half. Draw and cut out a piece of paper 1 inch by 6¾ inches. Tape the strip between the two halves of the circle, being careful to line up the center lines on the halves. You should slightly round off the squared outside edges of this center strip using a French curve. They should not protrude more than $\frac{1}{16}$ inch. This should give you a 23-inch basic oval pattern. Measure around it to check your accuracy. Perfect accuracy depends on many factors, including the width of the pencil you use, your compass, etc. Always check your ovals by measuring around them with a tape measure before finalizing them. Erase and correct the patterns as necessary to get accurate ovals.

Now that you have this basic oval, you can make ovals in different sizes based on this pattern. Use this guide to get approximate sizes: To increase the oval to $23\frac{3}{4}$ inches, trace a line $\frac{1}{8}$ inch around the oval. To increase the new $23\frac{3}{4}$-inch oval to $24\frac{1}{2}$ inches, trace a line $\frac{1}{8}$ inch around the oval. To increase the $24\frac{1}{2}$-inch oval to 25 inches, trace a line $\frac{1}{8}$ inch around the oval.

To decrease the 23-inch oval to 22-$\frac{1}{4}$ inches, trace a line $\frac{1}{8}$ inch inside the oval. To decrease the $22\frac{1}{4}$-inch oval to $21\frac{1}{2}$ inches, trace a line $\frac{1}{8}$ inch inside it.

You can see how the slightest addition or subtraction from the oval will make a fairly significant size difference. I have not included a master oval pattern in this book, not only because of possible errors or distortion that it could receive in printing, but also because I think it is important for milliners to be able to make any size oval they need from scratch. It is good for a beginning milliner's basic pattern-making skills to get a hands-on feel for the geometry and math involved in making ovals and patterns from scratch.

Exercises

1. Make your own set of master oval patterns using the guidelines in this section. You should have a range of sizes from 21 inches around through 26 inches around at $\frac{1}{2}$-inch increments. Glue them to stiff cardboard and cut them out. Make sure they measure the correct size and that they are labeled.

2. Make a matching set of "negative space" ovals—rectangles of stiff cardboard that have oval holes in them like a brim. You can place these on actors' heads to determine both head size and the "regularity" of an actor's head oval. If an actor's head is unusually narrow from side-to-side, you will see it instantly. You can measure the distance with this tool, then make a special oval just for that actor.

3. Make a set of pillbox hat patterns in 1-inch head-size increments. Make one to fit a 21-inch head, a 22-inch head, and so on through a 26-inch head. Be sure to mark the center front and center back on all your pattern pieces, and label each piece with the type of hat and the size.

4. Copy one of your pillbox hat patterns onto new paper and try splitting and spreading it to make one side higher than the other, or the front tilted in one direction. You will have to make a new tip because you will be changing the dimensions of that oval. Can you think of other ways to split and spread a basic pillbox hat shape to make another hat?

4
Making a Pillbox Hat Pattern

$\mathcal{A}$ pillbox hat is simply a straight sideband and a flat tip that fits the head size of the wearer.

Making the Paper Pattern

The tools you will need are a sheet of brown craft paper at least 25 inches long, card stock, a sharp pencil, a right angle, a ruler, a French curve, and a compass. Note that it is vital that you keep your pencil very sharp so that you get very accurate results.

The Sideband

We'll start by drawing the sideband, which is a large rectangle. Near one long edge of the paper, draw a straight line that is 23 inches long and label it A (Figure 4.1).

Using a right angle, draw a 5-inch line extending up from each end of line A (Figure 4.2). Both lines should be at a perfect right angle to line A. Label one of the new lines B and the other C.

Draw a line from the end of line B to the end of line C. This line, which is parallel to line A, will also be 23 inches long. Label it D (Figure 4.3).

Label your pattern piece: Pillbox Sideband—23″.

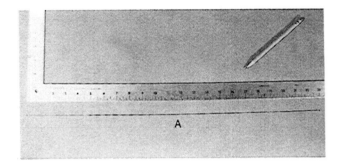

Figure 4.1 23-inch line labeled A.

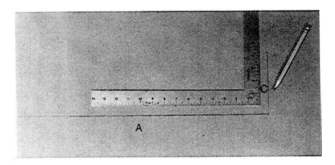

Figure 4.2 5-inch line labeled C.

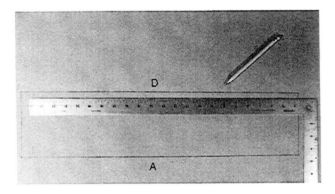

Figure 4.3 Line D.

The Tip

We'll make the tip using a good method of making an oval pattern. Make a dot about 8 inches above the sideband. Label the dot E. Using a compass set at $3\frac{3}{8}$ inches, make a circle using dot E as the center (Figure 4.4).

Measure down from dot E 1 inch and make a new dot, labeled F. Make another circle the same size using dot F as the center. You will end up with two overlapping circles (Figure 4.5).

Now connect the circles to make an oval. Use a ruler to draw a straight line on each side of the overlapping circles, connecting them. Label these lines G and H (Figure 4.6).

Use a ruler to find the center of line G and mark the center with a dot. Measure out from the dot at a right angle $\frac{1}{16}$ inch and make a new dot. Label it J. Repeat on the other side, measuring out from line H and labeling the new dot K.

Use a French curve to draw a curved line from the side of circle E through dot J and to the side of circle F. Do the same thing to the other side, blending the two circles by drawing a curved line from the side of circle E through dot K and to the side of circle F (Figure 4.7).

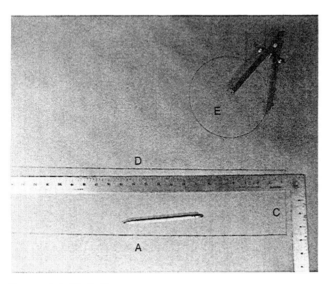

Figure 4.4 Circle E.

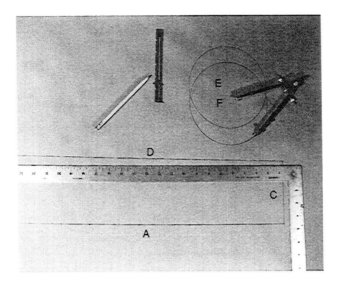

Figure 4.5 Overlapping circle F.

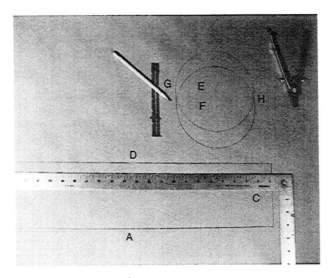

Figure 4.6 Lines G and H.

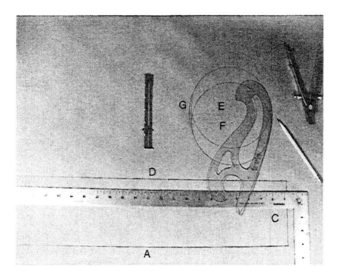

Figure 4.7 Using a French curve to complete the oval.

Mark the center front and center back of the oval. To find the center line, cut out the oval and fold it in half so that dots J and K are together (Figure 4.8). Crease the center. Unfold the pattern and, using a ruler, draw a line on the crease. Mark one end of this line CF for "center front" and the other end CB for "center back."

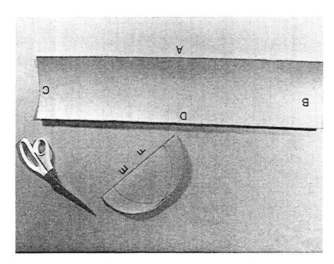

Figure 4.8 Oval folded with dots J and K together.

Check the circumference of your oval with a tape measure. If you need to, correct the oval until it measures a true 23 inches. Sometimes you'll end up with a slightly larger or slightly smaller oval. Even the smallest difference in the width of your pencil lead can make a big difference in your line. You can also make errors when cutting out a pattern, cutting too far inside or outside the line, or cutting so carelessly that the pattern ends up being nowhere near 23 inches. My advice: Precision matters.

Making a Card Stock Mock-up

Use your paper patterns to trace the pillbox pieces onto card stock. Be sure to mark the center front and center back. Cut the pieces out and label them. Tape the sideband edges B and C together to make a cylinder (Figure 4.9). Use small pieces of tape to insert the tip into the sideband, lining up seam B/C on the sideband with the center back of the tip (Figure 4.10). You usually want to put the seam in the center back of a hat so that the front of the hat remains smooth and unbroken.

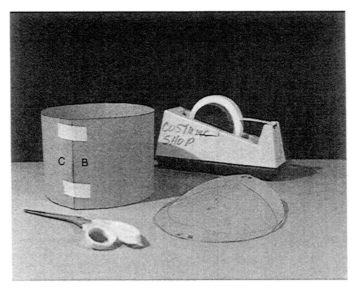

Figure 4.9 Sideband taped to make a cylinder.

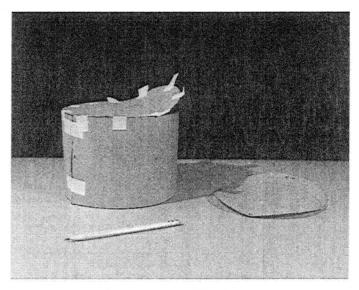

Figure 4.10 Tape the tip into the sideband.

If the tip and the sideband don't seem to fit together correctly, you have probably made one of the pieces too large or too small. Lay the pieces flat again and double-check your measurements. Remake the pattern if necessary. With practice, you'll have fewer and fewer errors.

Once the tip is in place, you have created a mock-up for a pillbox hat. This shape is the base for many kinds of hats, so save the pattern for later use. Put it in a large envelope and be sure to label the outside.

Adding a Brim

You can make a brim to add to your pillbox. With a brim attached, the sideband and tip of the basic pillbox become the hat's crown. First trace the tip pattern in the center of a new piece of paper at least 26 inches square. Mark the center front and center back. Use a ruler to measure out from the oval 3 inches (or whatever width you'd like the finished brim to be) all the way around, making dots at this measurement (Figure 4.11). Connect the dots using a French curve. Once you have drawn

Figure 4.11 Make dots around the oval.

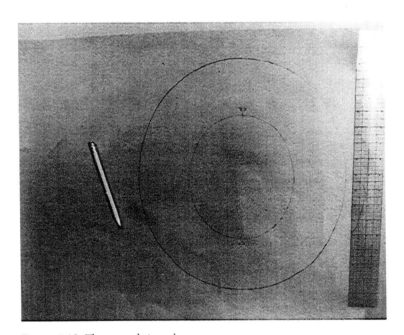

Figure 4.12 The outer brim edge.

Figure 4.13 Brim taped to the pillbox's head-size opening.

the outside of the brim edge (Figure 4.12), cut it out and tape it to the bottom of your pillbox, being sure to line up the center backs of brim and crown (Figure 4.13).

You'll typically want to keep your brims under 4 inches in width. Anything wider than that starts looking comical. There are exceptions, of course, such as when you are making a woman's large-brimmed Victorian hat. Even when making very large brims, there are things you can do to keep the actor's face out of the shadow cast by a brim. I have made hats that were wider by about an inch in the back and on the sides than in the front. Depending on the size of the theater in which your hats will be seen, you may be able to make subtle adjustments like this to create the effect of a large brim without blocking the actor's facial light as much. Experienced milliners know that a hat brim should be as narrow as possible for use on the stage. This isn't as much of a problem in the movie business since camera angles and lighting can be much more flexible than stage lighting. Stage directors, actors, and lighting designers will appreciate a narrow brim. There is an art to making a brim that suits both the aesthetic needs of the play or of the period and the practical concern of keeping the actor visible to the audience. Remember, "the play's the thing"—you want your hats to add to the production, not get in its way.

5
Making a Buckram Pillbox Hat

 $\mathcal{T}$ o make a pillbox hat from buckram, you'll need the following tools: buckram, pushpins, pencil, seam gauge, craft scissors, sewing machine, heavy-duty sewing machine needles, strong thread, millinery wire, wire cutters, masking tape, straight pins, safety goggles, a thick plasticized coating like Sculpt Or Coat, a small disposable paintbrush, and a hand-sewing needle. You'll use the pillbox pattern you already have.

Creating the Basic Structure

Roll out a piece of buckram and pin it to the table to hold it flat. Buckram has a natural curve in it from where it was rolled up. You will want to pay close attention to how you orient the pattern pieces to take advantage of this curve, rather than having to fight it. Place the sideband pattern piece against the buckram so that the finished piece will curl into an oval. I like to orient my tip pattern on the buckram so that the line from center front to center back follows the curve as well. You want to ensure that whatever physical stresses the left side of the tip is experiencing are the same on the right side. This will keep the hat symmetrical.

Once you have oriented the pattern pieces correctly on the buckram, pin them in place and trace around them with a sharp pencil (Figure 5.1). Be sure to mark CF CB. Don't use ink or markers, which can seep through the hat's fabric coverings.

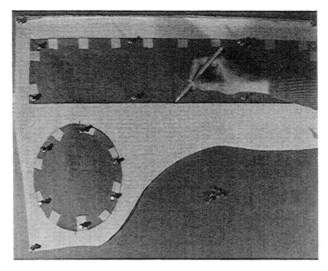

Figure 5.1 Tracing the pattern on the buckram.

Even if you are very careful, marker and ink can be activated by an actor's sweat and ruin an otherwise perfect hat. A reality of making garments is that people will sweat in them—and some will sweat profusely.

Unpin the pattern pieces. Using a seam gauge on the buckram, add a ½-inch seam allowance to the B and C edges of the sideband. Do not add seam allowance anywhere else on the sideband or on the tip. Using craft scissors (*not* your cloth scissors), cut out the sideband and tip.

Use your sewing machine to sew the center back seam on the sideband (Figure 5.2). Be sure there is a new sharp, sturdy needle in the machine. I like to use denim needles. Set the machine to do a very wide, very long zigzag stitch. Line up the sideband—you may pin it in place if you want, or use a little tape to hold it in place. (Be sure to place the pins or the tape so you don't sew over or through them.) Put the buckram under the presser foot. You may have to slightly distort the sideband to get it to go under the foot—just be careful not to permanently crease or damage it. Back-stitch at the beginning and end of your stitching to lock the stitch in place, just as you would when sewing fabric. Sew the seam and clip any hanging threads. (You will end up with a much better product if you clip all hanging threads as you go along.)

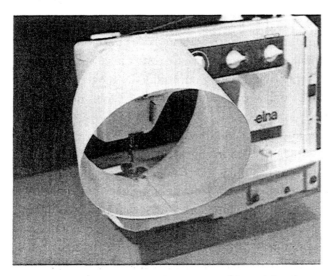

Figure 5.2 Sewing the center back seam of the sideband.

Adding Wire

When working with buckram, it is important to add millinery wire to the edges. This provides strength to the pieces and prevents the hat from stretching or distorting with wear.

> **Note:** Wear safety goggles when sewing over wire. If you accidentally get the piece off the center mark, the needle could hit the wire and break. Sewing machines sew with a lot of force, and needle shards can fly up at you with a lot of energy. Even a very experienced milliner should always wear eye protection while sewing over wire.

Get your millinery wire and remove the small ties that keep it bundled together. Hold the wire bundle with one hand while you do this so it won't spring apart into a tangled mess. Once you have the ties removed (I cut them off with wire cutters), slowly and gently ease up on your grip and allow the wire to uncoil in a controlled manner in your hand. Uncoil millinery wire only as you need a roll—usually there is no reason to have more than one roll untied and uncoiled at a time.

Measure around the oval of your cut-out buckram tip—remember, it should be 23 inches around—and correct it if necessary. Use your wire cutters to cut a piece of millinery wire that is 2 inches longer than you need—you can cut off any excess later. Be careful not to bend the wire. We'll be working with the natural curve in the wire, much as we worked with natural curve in the buckram. (There is more about working with wire later in this book.)

When you sew wire to the edge of buckram, the goal is to zigzag over the wire allowing one side of the zigzag stitch to catch the buckram and the other side of the stitch to catch only the thread, overcasting the material and sewing nothing at all. Practice on a scrap piece of buckram with a scrap of wire. It may seem odd or difficult at first, especially if you are used to sewing fabric, but it isn't really too different from garment sewing. Go slowly until you get the hang of it. You may find that you need to slightly uncurl the millinery wire as you sew. Do so by repeatedly running your hand over the wire, stroking it with you finger and applying slight pressure. This will bend the wire gradually and smoothly without causing bends or kinks.

To attach the wire to the edge of the tip, line up the end of the wire at the CB mark on the buckram. You may want to use a few pieces of masking tape to hold the wire in place until you get the hang of this. Remove the tape before you sew over or through it. Be sure the wire is exactly on the edge of the buckram, not on top or underneath. For now, let the excess wire hang freely at the back. Place the tip under the presser foot of the sewing machine, which should still be set up to sew a wide, long zigzag stitch. Line up the wire with the center guide mark on the presser foot or the center mark on the sewing machine. As long as you manipulate the tip so that the wire stays on the center mark, the machine will sew on the left and the right side of the wire (Figure 5.3).

When you get about half of the wire sewn to the edge of the buckram, stop and cut off any excess wire at the center back of the tip. Leave a slight overlap, about ¾ inch. It's a good idea to wait to this point in the process to shorten the wire so that you don't end up making it too short and discovering the problem only after you have the whole wire sewn down.

Continue sewing the wire to the tip. When you get to the overlap, stop sewing and shorten the stitch length to a little above the shortest setting. Then, working very slowly, sew the overlapping section of wire to the wire that's already attached to the buckram. Cover the entire overlap with stitching. This little overlap might cause the slightest bump, but it won't be noticeable in the finished hat.

Figure 5.3 Sewing wire to the edge of a tip using a wide zigzag.

You can also use a wire joiner, a fastener that is specifically meant to join millinery wire to itself (available from millinery suppliers). These are small metal tubes that are meant to be slipped over the ends of the wire and crimped to hold them in place. I do not like wire joiners, as I have yet to see one that was the correct size for the wire it was joining and I have yet to see one stay fastened—over time they always seem to pop apart. They tend to rust, and they often allow the millinery wire to spin inside the fastener, which adds instability to the hat. It's just too likely that using a wire joiner will cause a future problem. If you must use one, make sure you have the correct size. Most importantly, use epoxy glue on both ends of the wire, so that you are gluing the joiner in place. Epoxy, available at hardware stores, will glue metal to metal—millinery glue will not. Once the ends are glued, crimp the joiner over the ends. Stitch over the joiner, fastening it and the wire to the buckram.

Wire the tip edge and bottom edge of the sideband the same way you wired the tip, making sure you place the wire on the exact edge of the buckram, not on the inside or outside flat surface. Be sure to line up the stitched overlap (or wire joiner) at the center back.

Figure 5.4 Using Sculpt Or Coat to adhere the wire to the buckram

Once you have wired all of your pieces, you need to permanently fuse the wire to the buckram. Get a small paintbrush and a plasticized coating like Sculpt Or Coat (Figure 5.4). Many glues commonly used in costume shops are too wet to use for this step. The moisture actually activates the sizing in the buckram and the fabric's stiffness and shape are lost. I recommend Sculpt Or Coat because it is not too wet, it is nontoxic, it is incredibly versatile, and it dries clear and strong. Completely coat the wire, making sure to fill in any tiny gaps and spreading the adhesive out onto the buckram at least ½ inch. The goal is to cover all of the wire and all of the stitching holding the wire to the buckram. Make sure to apply the Sculpt Or Coat smoothly. You don't need to put it on too thickly. I usually use my fingers to smooth it out. Allow the parts to dry completely. Drying time will vary with temperature and humidity. You can use a hair dryer to speed up drying time if necessary.

Assemble the Buckram Base

Put your dry pieces together, making sure to line up the CB marks. With a needle and thread, attach the tip to the sideband by using a whipstitch to sew the wire on the tip to the wire on the sideband (Figure 5.5). It is not necessary to stitch through the buckram, and in fact you want to try not to do so. Stitches in the buckram could eventually tear through it and weaken the structure of the hat. It may be difficult to stitch through the Sculpt Or Coat. Use your thimble or needle-nose pliers to help

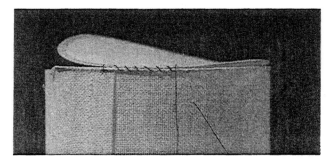

Figure 5.5 Using a whipstitch to attach the tip to the sideband.

push the needle through. Once you have the tip and the sideband joined, fuse the seams together with a little more Sculpt Or Coat on the inside and outside of the hat. Allow this to dry. The base of your hat it done!

Covering the Hat

Many people have asked me about it, and many people have tried to do it, but let me begin this section by emphatically stating that if you want a nicely made hat, you cannot simply make a cover on the sewing machine, turn it inside out, then pop it onto the hat base. Think of covering a hat as similar to putting fabric on a couch. It is the same as upholstering a sofa, not simply covering it with a slipcover. If you try to take too many shortcuts when covering a hat with fabric, you'll end up with a lumpy hat. Good-quality millinery is an art done one piece of fabric at a time, like good upholstery. In this section, we'll use the sewing machine some and I will guide you through several acceptable shortcuts—but don't try to do it all on a sewing machine. Learn to enjoy the parts of hatmaking that require good old-fashioned, time-consuming craft.

Choose a medium-weight fabric that is visually interesting, like a thin brocade or medium-weight silk. Fabric with a pattern or an interesting texture will look better than a visually flat fabric. Pin your pattern to the fabric and mark a ⅝-inch seam allowance all around it using a seam gauge and a sharp pencil. If the pencil mark doesn't show, use tailor's chalk (Figure 5.6). At the B and C edges of the sideband piece, add an extra inch. This extra couple of inches will give you room to expand. Cut out the pieces of fabric with your cloth-only scissors.

Figure 5.6 Using tailor's chalk to mark a seam allowance.

Cover the buckram tip with your tip fabric, lining up the CB and CF marks. Pin or tape the tip fabric in place and begin sewing the seam allowance down to the side-band (Figure 5.7). Start sewing at the center back and work your way around the hat about ⅛ inch down from the top edge using a basic stab stitch (in and out, in

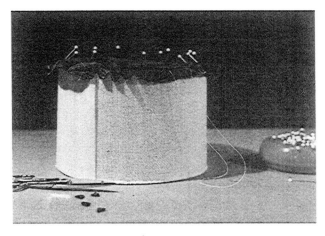

Figure 5.7 Attaching the fabric tip to the buckram.

and out). These stitches will eventually get covered, so don't worry too much about how they look. Just make sure the fabric is smooth and snug on the tip of the hat. When you are done, use your fabric-only scissors to clip the seam allowance. Clip notches out of the seam allowance to allow it to lay flat and smooth against the side of the hat.

Wrap the sideband fabric around the hat with the wrong side out. Pinch it together at the center back and pin it snugly there (Figure 5.8). Slide the sideband fabric off the hat with the pins still in place and sew it together on the machine with a straight stitch. Be sure to backstitch at the beginning and end of the seam. Press the seam open with a steam iron. Trim the seam allowance, but not too close to the stitching line— leave ¼-inch seam allowance on each side of the stitching, or ⅝ inch if your fabric unravels easily. You might trim your seam allowance with pinking shears to further inhibit fraying. While you are still at the iron, turn the top edge of the sideband fabric down about ¼ inch and press it. This pressed edge will get stitched to the fabric tip. Turn the sideband fabric right side out and slide it over the hat, making sure to line up the center back, and making sure that the pressed edge is at the tip of the hat.

Figure 5.8 Sideband fabric wrapped around the hat inside out.

Figure 5.9 Sideband fabric pinned to the tip

You can use a ruler like a shoehorn to help you slide the sideband on. Pin the tip edge together (Figure 5.9). Hand stitch the seam using a slipstitch, making sure your stitches don't show (Figure 5.10). Be sure to use small stitches, one every ³⁄₈ inch or so. Precision and neatness will make or break this step of the project.

Once the tip and the sideband are sewn together, you are ready to finish the bottom edge. You have two options here: Fold the bottom edge under to the inside of the hat, which will decrease the head size slightly, or fold the bottom seam allowance under the sideband fabric on the outside of the buckram sideband. If you choose the second option, be sure to put the fold of the fabric ever-so-slightly lower than the bottom edge of the fabric so that you can sew the lining to it later. Whichever option you choose, pin the fabric in place at the bottom edge of the hat. Pull it down so it's snug but not straining. You never want to construct a hat with so much tension that it is likely to develop "worry lines" from the stress. Hand sew the bottom in place with a simple stab stitch about ¹⁄₂ inch up from the bottom of the hat (Figure 5.11). Be sure the stitches are tiny—virtually invisible—on the out-

Figure 5.10 Slip stitching the sideband to the tip.

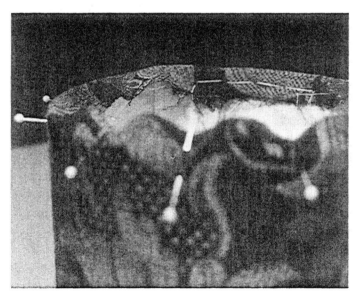

Figure 5.11 Sewing the bottom edge to the hat.

side of the hat. You can make longer stitches inside—they won't be seen when the hat is done.

Once the outside of the hat is covered, you are ready to add a lining and trim.

Lining the Hat

A professional-looking hat will have a lining. This creates a nicely finished hat, but adds more than just visual appeal. A lining has several functions. It hides seams or stitching on the inside of the crown. It keeps the hat from tangling the wearer's hairstyle. It can make a hat more comfortable to wear. It often makes a hat sturdier. And, frankly, a well-made and professionally finished costume stands a better chance than a poorly made costume of being well cared for by actors and wardrobe crews.

Choosing Fabric

Lining fabrics are sold in all fabric stores, and are typically chosen to be thinner than the fabric of the garment they are lining. Pick a color that is less colorful than the hat you are lining. I use black whenever I can, or sometimes gray or off-white if the hat is a very light color. The costume designer may choose a lining for you; if not, ask for his or her preferences. Remember, you almost never want the inside of a hat to be more visually interesting than the outside.

The Lining Trick

This is a quick and easy technique for making a hat lining using your existing pillbox hat pattern. Begin by making the tip. Trace the tip piece of the pillbox pattern onto your lining fabric, leaving about 1 inch all the way around in which to add a seam allowance. Remove the pattern and use a seam gauge to mark a ⅝-inch seam allowance all around it. Be sure to mark the center front and center back of the tip. Cut out the piece. You may want to machine stitch a label to the tip toward the center back at this point, making sure not to put it in the seam allowance. It is easier to write the actor's name, the show, etc., on the label before it is sewn into the hat.

Now trace the sideband, adding 1 inch along the bottom edge (the A edge) (Figure 5.12). Mark a ⅝-inch seam allowance all around the remaining edges. Cut out the piece.

Pin the B and C edges together (Figure 5.13). Stitch them together and press the seam open. Pin the lining tip and sideband together, making sure to line up the cen-

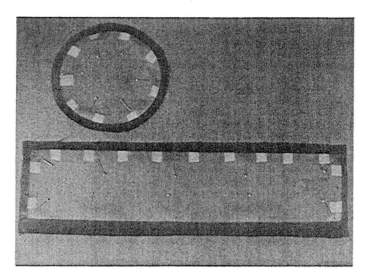

Figure 5.12 Lining tip and sideband with seam allowances added.

Figure 5.13 Lining sideband pinned together at center back, ready to be stitched.

ter back seam of the sideband with the CB mark on the tip (Figure 5.14). Stitch them together. Put the lining over an ironing ham and press the seam flat from the back side. I like to press the entire seam (between the tip and sideband) down against the sideband so that the inner tip fits smoothly against the crown.

Iron a grosgrain ribbon into a slight curve. You can do this by manipulating the ribbon with one hand and ironing with the other, pulling the ribbon into a crescent as you iron (Figure 5.15). Be sure to use steam, and be careful not to scorch the ribbon. Practice on a scrap piece of ribbon.

When you have enough curved ribbon to go around the head-size opening with about 1 inch of overlap, pin the ribbon into the hat all around the opening, with the overlap at the center back (Figure 5.16). Put your pins fairly close together, and make sure the ribbon is very smooth against the hat. Where the ribbon overlaps at the center back, fold one end of the ribbon under, then pin the two ends together, making sure not to pin the ribbon to the hat. Remove the ribbon from the hat, leaving it

Figure 5.14 Lining sideband and tip pinned together, ready to be stitched.

Figure 5.15 Ironing grosgrain ribbon into a slight curve.

Figure 5.16 Ribbon pinned in place, with ends pinned together.

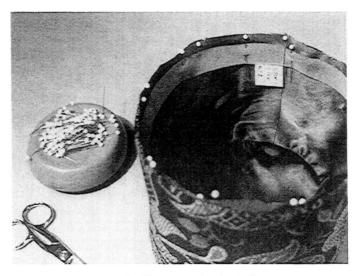

Figure 5.17 Lining and ribbon pinned into the hat.

pinned to itself. Machine stitch the ribbon loop together and press the seam open. Trim away the excess seam allowance, leaving about ¼ inch on each side of the seam.

Put the lining into the hat, making sure to line up the center back seams. Pin it in a few places. Put the head-size ribbon in the hat and pin it to the lining (Figure 5.17).

This is the time to make sure the lining and the ribbon are oriented correctly, and that they are pinned to each other. Once they are, remove them from the hat, making sure to keep them pinned together (Figure 5.18). Machine stitch them together with a straight stitch. Sew the grosgrain ribbon to the lining along the top edge of the ribbon (the edge that will be toward the tip of the crown). If you look closely at your grosgrain ribbon, you'll notice that it has a small groove along the edge. Use this groove as your sewing guideline, and make sure you use a thread color that matches the ribbon. If this step is done well, you will hardly notice the stitching. I usually start my stitching at the center back. Once you have the lining and the ribbon stitched together, you may need to press them to make sure they are flat.

You will notice that there is extra lining sticking out from the bottom of the ribbon. Clip the extra lining on the back of the ribbon, about half way down the rib-

Figure 5.18 Lining with ribbon pinned to it being removed from the hat.

bon—you don't want to trim it too closely to the stitching line (Figure 5.19). This should leave you with no lining edges showing on the right side of the lining.

Put the lining back into the hat. If you need to glue the tip in place, do so now. Pin the head-size ribbon into place, making sure to line up the center back seams. Using a slip stitch, sew the ribbon to the hat along the bottom edge (Figure 5.20). You may want to use a curved needle. A good milliner's hand stitching can hardly be seen even close up—be meticulous and make little stitches. Once you get the hang of top-quality small stitching, you will be able to do it quickly. As with anything, you will get better with practice.

The Finishing Touch

For a nice finishing touch, add a small bow to the back of the hat on the inner center back seam. I like to use midi-braid or a similar-size ribbon that matches the color of the lining. Tie a tiny bow the way you tie a shoe lace and stitch it through the center knot on the top edge of the head-size ribbon. This bow has a very real function,

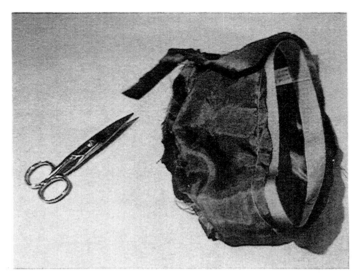

Figure 5.19 Excess lining being trimmed away behind the ribbon.

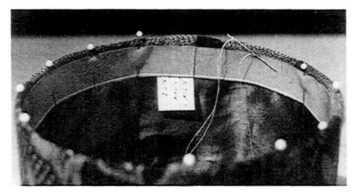

Figure 5.20 Sewing the ribbon edge into the hat.

in that it can help your actors find the back of the hat when they are onstage. I have been in many dress rehearsals where actors put their hats on backwards because they weren't sure which was the front and which was the back. What may seem obvious to you may not be so obvious to others. Save the day by always putting in a CB-indicator bow.

Exercises

1. Practice ironing grosgrain ribbon into a curve. See how much of a curve you can achieve without any wrinkles in the ribbon. Use good-quality grosgrain, which is called French belting.

2. Make pillbox patterns for a range of sizes, from 21 inches through 26 inches. Use the head oval patterns you already have as a basis for the tips. Make the sidebands at least 2½ inches tall. Do not make them any taller than 4 inches. Be sure to label every piece, and mark CB and CF on each tip.

3. Start your own hat research collection. Find as many pictures as you can of hats from various periods. Good sources include portrait paintings and photographs and tomb paintings. You should already have some pictures from earlier exercises to start you out. Divide your research collection into various time periods, then subdivide each time period into a men's section and a women's section. Find as many examples as you can of the basic pillbox shape, the fez or truncated cone shape, and the cone shape. (If you find other shapes, go ahead and include them.) Note on the bottom of each picture any information you might need later, such as the historic time period depicted, the source of the material, and the source region or country.

6
Making a Cloth Pillbox Hat

This section takes you through the process of making a simple cloth pillbox hat using the pattern you made earlier. Most millinery requires that you develop strong sewing skills. Some hats, like this pillbox, can be made entirely on the sewing machine—except for 3 inches of hand sewing. Use a medium-weight cotton fabric, something with a little stiffness to it. The photos show a bold geometric print fabric and a satin lining.

Lay your fabric out on your cutting table and make sure it is flat. Lay the lining fabric on top of the outer fabric, making sure the grain of both fabrics is in the same direction. Pin the two pattern pieces (the sideband and the tip) on top of both layers of the fabric with straight pins (Figure 6.1). Make sure the pins catch both layers so that they don't move around as you cut out the pieces. Use a seam gauge to mark a ⅝-inch seam allowance around both pieces. Draw the seam allowance on the top layer and cut both layers out using the top one as a guide—there is no reason to mark it on both layers. Be sure to mark the center front and center back on your pieces, or cut a small notch in the fabric to indicate them. Cut out both layers.

With the fabrics right sides together, use the sewing machine to straight stitch along one long edge of the sideband, sewing it to the lining fabric (Figure 6.2). Use a medium-length stitch and thread that matches the outer fabric. With a steam iron, press the seam allowance open so that your fabric matches the illustration (Figure 6.2). Here's a good trick: Fold the pieces so that the lining starts about ⅛ inch up

Figure 6.1 Sideband and tip patterns pinned to fabric.

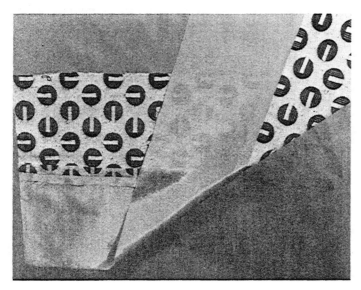

Figure 6.2 Lining and outer fabric sewn together along bottom edge of sideband.

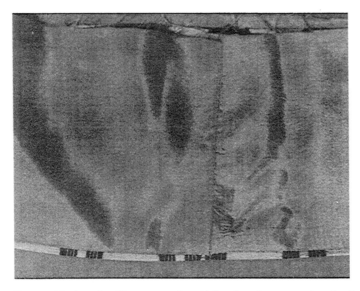

Figure 6.3 Sew the CB seam on the sideband and press so that the lining starts ⅛″ up from the bottom edge.

from the bottom and press again. This will create a fold in the outer fabric and will recess the lining on the inside of the hat (Figure 6.3).

Unfold the piece and place the short sides together, with the fabric's right sides together. Pin together. Make sure you are lining up the new fold and bottom edges you just made in the fabric. Machine stitch the seam through the outer fabric and continue on across the lining fabric. Press this short seam open with a steam iron, then press the bottom crease again where it intersects the center back seam you just made.

Turn the sideband inside out. Pin the tip to the outer fabric of the sideband, first lining up the center front and pinning it, then lining up the center back and pinning that (Figure 6.4 and Figure 6.5). For now, disregard the lining fabric. Sew the tip onto the top edge of the sideband, making sure that you are not accidentally catching the lining fabric. Put the hat on a pressing ham or sleeve-pressing board and press the seam, making sure that both seam allowances are pressed down against the sideband.

To add stability and a decorative element to the hat, stitch the seam allowances down all around the tip, following the seam with the presser foot, about ⅜ inch from

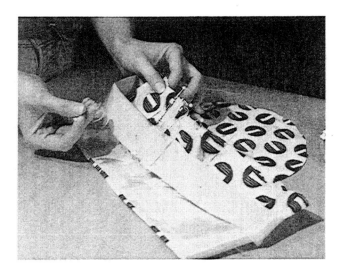

Figure 6.4 Line up the center back of the tip to the center back of the sideband and continue pinning around the tip.

Figure 6.5 The tip pinned into the sideband, ready to be stitched. Once stitched, fold the seam allowance down and topstitch it in place.

the seam. Use your fingers to open the seam fully as you sew, and keep the lining fabric out of the way.

Pull the lining out and turn the hat inside out. Pin the lining tip to the top of the sideband lining, again starting by pinning the center front and center back. Distribute the remaining fullness around as you pin. After the lining is pinned, sew the seam leaving a 3-inch opening at the center back. Turn the hat right side out through the 3-inch opening and press the lining seam open if needed.

Finish the hat by hand sewing the 3-inch opening. If you like, sew a grosgrain ribbon on the inside bottom edge of the sideband. In this case, a ribbon would be more of a sweatband and not very necessary for strength or stability. You may also decide to add a decorative top stitch around the bottom edge of the hat through both layers of fabric, about ½ inch up from the edge (Figure 6.6).

Figure 6.6 The finished soft pillbox hat.

7
Making a Draped Buckram Hat

The pillbox you just made is basically all flat construction with buckram. You laid out all the pieces with a pencil and ruler much as you would with a garment. Remember, buckram is a loosely woven fabric that has been impregnated with water-soluble sizing to stiffen it. You can get buckram in single weight and double (crown) weight, and it is very strong and lightweight, making it perfect for this kind of flat-patterning construction.

But buckram has another wonderful quality because of the water-soluble sizing—if you get it wet, it will activate the sizing and soften the material. Then you can drape the buckram on any form. When it dries, it will stiffen and remain in this new shape.

To drape a buckram crown, first prepare your work area by putting down a plastic drop cloth. I like to keep an old towel handy to mop up splashed or spilled water. Next, find a shape to use as your form. You might use a football, a plastic mixing bowl, or a head block. If you use a head block or any other item that the sizing might stick to and ruin, cover it with plastic wrap, using cellophane tape to hold it in place. If you use a head block, make sure no water can get onto the wood. If you are using a form that doesn't have a stable flat bottom, find a way of making it stable and able to stand on its own.

Once you've set up your form, cut a piece of buckram about 12 inches square. Fill a deep sink or a large kettle with warm water. After you turn the water off and, when the water has stopped moving, immerse the buckram (Figure 7.1). It is

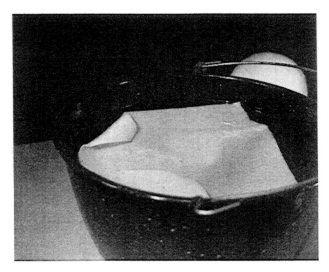

Figure 7.1 Buckram square in a pan of warm water.

important that you do not put the buckram into the stream of the water. This can wash off the sizing, and you want to leave as much sizing in the buckram as possible. Keep feeling the buckram. As soon as it starts going limp, take it out of the water and drape it over your form, smoothing out wrinkles as best you can.

As soon as you have draped the buckram, you have twenty minutes or so before it starts drying too much to work with. Surround the buckram on the form with a rubber band or tie a piece of elastic snugly around it. Manipulate the buckram, pulling at the bottom edges and working with the bias grain to smooth it out. If you are working on a head block or other form that can be pinned, pin the elastic in place with pushpins (Figure 7.2). Once the buckram is smooth, allow it to dry overnight. If you like, once it has dried a few hours you can take craft scissors and trim off the excess buckram hanging below the elastic band. This will make removing the dried buckram a little easier later.

The next day, remove the buckram from the form. Sometimes it comes off easily; sometimes it is stubborn and needs some work to remove. Use a metal corset stay (if you are in a costume shop and have access to one) to slide up under the buckram

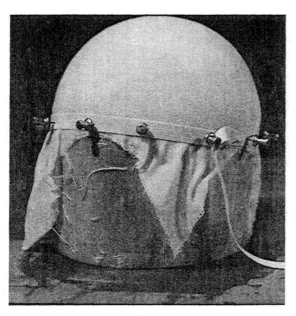

Figure 7.2 Wet buckram stretched over a wooden head block, with elastic band and pins holding it in place.

to loosen it. If the buckram is on top of a plastic wrap layer, unfasten the wrap at the bottom of the form and use it to help pull the buckram off the form. Get a friend to help pull it off if you need help. Remember not to crush the shape as you remove it!

When it is off the form, use craft scissors to trim the bottom edge to the desired shape. You might decide that this bottom edge needs to be reinforced with millinery wire. Attach the wire as you did to the edges of the pillbox hat. Make sure the wire is on the very edge of the buckram and that your center back is properly lined up (Figure 7.3). Fuse the wire to the buckram with Sculpt Or Coat (Figure 7.4) and allow it to dry thoroughly.

How you cover the shape will depend on the shape you have chosen. Make the lining first, using the same form you draped the buckram over. Drape the lining fabric over the form, then smooth it out and pinch out any fullness. Pin the fullness out to create seams in the fabric, then stitch the seams in place. Put the fabric over a pressing ham or sleeve-pressing board and press the seams open. Trim away excess fabric on each side of your stitches, but don't go too close to the stitching line.

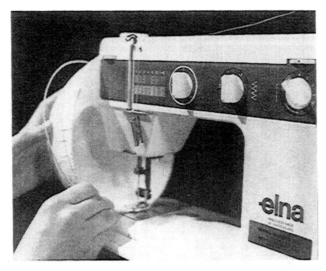

Figure 7.3 Sewing wire onto the edge of a draped buckram shape.

Figure 7.4 Applying Sculpt Or Coat to the wire.

Use the buckram shape you made to create the outer covering. Drape the outer covering fabric wrong side out over the shape and pin it in until it is smooth. Remove it from the shape and machine stitch the pinned-in seams. Press the seams open over a ham. Turn the cover right side out and slide it over the buckram hat. Finish the bottom edges as you did when making the pillbox hat.

Exercises

1. Practice covering a head block with different kinds of fabric. The goal is to make a cover that follows the shape closely and smoothly, with as few seams as possible. Start with a very thick, heavy fabric, like denim. Then make covers out of a sheer, delicate fabric like chiffon, a stretchy fabric, and muslin or some other medium-weight stable fabric.

2. Often when making a hat, you will make a very basic shape and apply other shapes to it to achieve the final design. Find a small glass or plastic container that might be appropriate for one of these "applied" shapes. Drape the small shape with soaked buckram, then allow it to dry. Remove the buckram and trim off the edges. Find two other small objects that would be suitable for applied shapes and repeat the process. Cover the three shapes with fabric.

3. Get a piece of buckram and draw a circle on it that is at least 12 inches in diameter. Mark the center. Cut the circle out with craft scissors. Place the edges of the dry buckram over a head block. Using steam, shape the edges and keep working them with your hands and more steam to make all of the edges curl up (Figures 7.5 and 7.6). With practice you will be able to make the outer

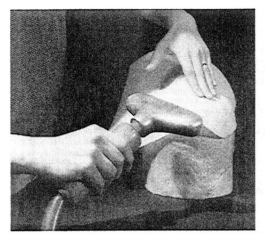

Figure 7.5 Steaming buckram over a form.

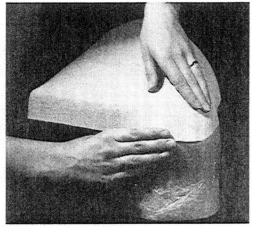

Figure 7.6 Using the hands to shape the steamed buckram.

edge curl up all around like a shallow bowl. Once you have achieved the shape you want, sew wire to the edge to hold it in place and paint on Sculpt Or Coat it to make it permanent. Use this same technique to create a shaped brim for a hat.

4. Make a hat using the brim from exercise 3. Make an appropriately sized crown to go with it using a draped buckram form. Once you have your crown done and the bottom edge of it properly wired, center the crown on the brim. Trace around it on the brim, then cut out the head-size opening. Wire this edge as you have wired other edges. Once it is dry, hand sew the crown and brim together using the same technique you used to sew the buckram tip and side-band together.

5. Take the hat you just made and cover it with fabric and make a lining for it.

8
Making a Wire-Framed Hat

Many hats are either so large or such an odd shape that you will want to minimize the weight and maximize the strength of the structure. One of the best ways to do this is to use millinery wire, rather than buckram, for the hat's base. You can construct quite large and complicated hats with wire using the techniques in this section. Wire is also useful to make a sheer hat, such as one that's covered with chiffon or lace. It works exceptionally well for large-brimmed Victorian ladies' hats.

Before I start guiding you through the project, let me begin with my "wire philosophy"—guidelines for working with millinery wire.

Working with Wire

Millinery wire is specifically made for use in hatmaking. It comes in a variety of gauges—the smaller the gauge number, the thicker and stronger the wire. The wire is covered or wrapped with thread. Millinery wire is sold in small coiled bundles tied together with small wires. Millinery wire has a tendency to curve. This is a good quality—you can make the curve in the wire work for you.

To untie the millinery wire and to begin using it, first put on your safety goggles. Hold the coil firmly in one hand. Keep in mind that it's wound like a spring and you need to release the tension in the coil before you use it. Use wire cutters to remove the small ties that keep it bundled together. Continue to hold the wire bundle with one hand while you do this so it won't spring apart into a tangled mess. Once you have the restraining ties removed, slowly and gently ease up on your grip and allow the wire to uncoil in a controlled manner in your hand. Uncoil millinery wire only as you need a roll—usually there is no reason to have more than one roll untied and uncoiled at a time. Once the wire has uncoiled, you might want to keep it on a pegboard—I find that this storage method keeps the wire cleaner than if it lies on my table. You could also keep your wire in a plastic bag to keep the dust off.

I have worked with costume crafters in the past and watched in disbelief as they tried to make a hat by straightening out the wire before working with it. There will be places on a hat where you will need some straight pieces, but as a general rule, do not straighten out the wire. It makes no sense to straighten it out only to bend it into a circle later. If you need a larger arc than you find in the wire naturally, use your hand to relax the curve in the wire by running the wire through your fingers while your thumb gently presses it into a broader arc. Use the same method to straighten wire when you need a straight piece. A word of warning—make sure your hands are clean before you begin to manipulate wire. Even if the hat will eventually be covered with fabric, you want to keep the wire frame as clean as possible.

Sometimes you might work on a very complex shape with curves going in several different directions. When that is the case, let the natural curve of the wire follow the dominant curve of the shape you are making (even if you have relaxed the natural curve in the wire). It is advantageous to avoid working against the natural curve in the wire whenever possible.

Millinery wire has another property that is important to understand, what I call the plane of the wire. If you look at a roll of millinery wire from one angle, you'll notice right away that it is perfectly round. If you turn the roll sideways and look again, you'll see that from that angle it is relatively flat. This flatness is the plane of the wire, and it is critical that you pay close attention to it as you work. If you ever work on a wire-frame hat without paying close attention to the plane of the wire, you will end up with a lot of crookedness or twisting in the hat. If your wire hats seem to want to torque into some odd shape that you didn't intend, some of your pieces of wire are out of plane.

Making a Basic Shape

This exercise will introduce you to several fundamental wire-working techniques. Pretend you need a piece of wire that will go across one side of the brim, bend and go up the side of the crown, bend and go across the tip, bend and go down the other side of the crown, then bend and finish the other side of the brim.

Estimate what each measurement should be. Perhaps the brim is 3 inches across (which gives you 6 inches), the crown is 2 inches high (which gives you 4 inches), and the tip is 4 inches across. Allow 2 inches for bends and to finish off the wire. Using wire cutters, cut a piece of millinery wire that is 16 inches long (6 + 4 + 4 + 2 = 16).

Use your fingers to straighten the wire. It may take some time. It is most important that you end up with a very smooth piece of wire. Be a perfectionist. If your wire has lumpy or crooked places, keep smoothing it until it is perfect.

Once the wire is straight, find the center of the piece and mark it with a pencil. Measure from the center and mark each place on the wire where you need to make a bend. Mark the outside edges of the brim. You should have about an inch on each end of the wire beyond the brim edge. Now, using needle-nose pliers, bend the wire into the hat's profile shape (Figure 8.1). Using needle-nose pliers gives you a much more accurate and crisp bend.

To check to see how well you did, lay the piece on a flat surface like the tabletop (Figure 8.2). Does the piece lay perfectly flat? Is there any place where the wire is not flat against the table?

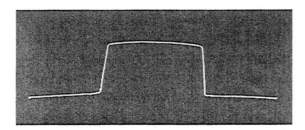

Figure 8.1 Wire hat profile.

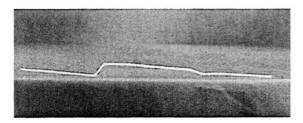

Figure 8.2 Wire profile on a flat surface—the piece is not flat against the table.

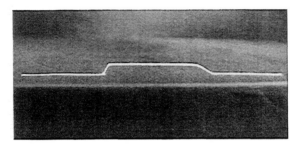

Figure 8.3 Wire profile perfectly flat against the table.

Pay special attention to the corners that you bent. If the piece is not perfectly flat before you put it into your hat structure, you will be adding crookedness and torque to the hat, and it may never retain the shape you intended. How do you fix this problem? If the piece is extremely not flat, you may need to start with a new piece of wire. If it is only slightly not flat, you can keep manipulating it with your hands or pliers until it will lay flat on the table (Figure 8.3). Getting the wire to be flat quickly will come with practice.

Always test your pieces with this "table test" to check if they are in the correct plane. If you learn to work with the plane and curve of the wire, there is no end to the hats you can create.

Wire-Joining Methods

As you work with perfectly curved and perfectly flat wire you are going to need some way to fasten the wire to itself. What follows are my preferred methods of joining wire.

There are several kinds of joints in wire construction, most of which use some kind of fastening to hold the wires together where they meet.

- ➲ the end-to-end joint, where two wire ends meet and join
- ➲ the overlapping or parallel joint, where one wire meets another with a small section of the first overlapping and joining the second
- ➲ the encircling joint, where one wire meets another wire and wraps around it to join it
- ➲ the cross joint, where two wires crisscross each other and are fastened together where they intersect

One method of joining wires end-to-end is the wire joiner, a small metal sleeve. This device is supposed to be inserted over two ends of wire and crimped tightly over the ends to hold them. I do not like wire joiners for several reasons. They often rust, they seldom stay together with wear, and they allow the millinery wire to rotate inside the joiner, making the joint unstable. If you use wire joiners, which are available from millinery suppliers, make sure you get the correct size for your wire. Use epoxy inside both ends of the joiner to permanently hold the wire and to prevent it from rotating. Make sure the joiner is properly crimped, and put the wire aside to dry before installing it in your hat frame. I would even coat the outside of the joiner with Sculpt Or Coat to ensure that the metal will not rust down the road.

To make an encircling joint, use your needle-nose pliers to simply loop one wire around the other. You can squeeze the loop with the pliers to get a very snug joint that doesn't easily allow the wire to slip through. I don't recommend this joint since it is difficult to do well and it is bulky, but there are times when it is just the right solution.

The other methods of joining wire require a tie wire, a separate piece of smaller wire, to tie the joints together. Millinery suppliers sell a product called tie wire that is similar to millinery wire in that it is coated or wrapped with thread. I do not like this tie wire as it is very thick and ends up giving you a bulky joint that is not particularly sturdy. It is useful for other purposes, such as for trimming hats, so if you already have some, don't throw it away. If you go to your local craft store or craft section of a department store, you can find a very thin-gauge inexpensive metal wire, sometimes called beading wire. It usually comes wound on a spool or around a small piece of flat cardboard. This wire is about the same thickness as thread, and comes in different colors. I usually use silver, but the gold color can be used decoratively. If you can't find beading wire, look in a hardware store or craft specialty store for any very thin metal wire the thickness of thread. Once you find a wire you like, stock up so you aren't always having to go shopping to get more!

To make the overlapping, or parallel, joint (Figure 8.4), begin by cutting a piece of tie wire at least 6 inches long. Overlap the millinery wires about 1½ inches and pinch them together in one hand. Place one end of the tie wire against one end of the millinery wire, keeping the tie parallel with the millinery wire joint. Pinch the tie wire and millinery wire together with one hand. With the other hand, begin wrapping the long free end of the tie wire around the joint and back over the pinched end of the tie wire itself. Be sure to keep lots of pressure on the tie wire and

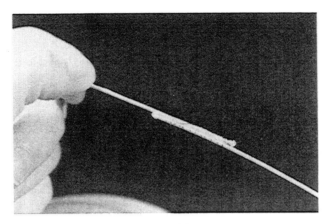

Figure 8.4 Overlapping, or parallel, joint.

wrap it tightly, using pliers if necessary. Wrap the wire tightly in place one or two times to get a good grip, then make each successive wrap at least $\frac{1}{16}$ inch apart from the previous one. Do not let your wrapping pile up on itself, but keep moving the wrapping wire down the length of the overlapping joint. When you reach the end, tuck the tie wire between the two pieces of millinery wire and cut off any excess. Make sure that the end of the tie wire is not sticking out at all—this could cause prob-

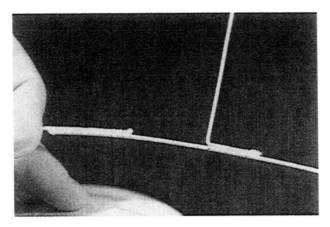

Figure 8.5 Right-angle joint, or T-joint.

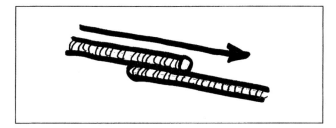

Figure 8.6 Tie wire laid parallel to millinery wires.

lems later when you try to cover the hat with fabric. Run your finger over it to make sure there are no exposed tie wire ends.

A variant of the overlapping joint is the right-angle joint, or T-joint (Figure 8.5). When one wire meets another at a right angle, leave about a 1-inch "tab" on one so that you can join them together. Bend the tab so that it is parallel to the wire it is joining, paying very close attention to the plane of the wire. Wrap the joint together with tie wire as described above. If your tab will be joining a curved piece of wire (like an outside brim edge), the tab should have a slight curve to match.

When I need an end-to-end joint, often I will instead leave myself an extra inch of wire to overlap. This creates an overlap joint instead of an end-to-end joint, which gives the finished structure a lot more strength. The overlap joint gets tied together as described above: You start the tie wire by laying it parallel to the millinery wires (Figure 8.6), then tightly wrap the tie wire back over itself (Figure 8.7), then wrap

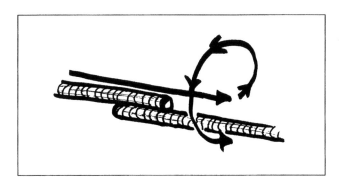

Figure 8.7 Tie wire wrapped back over itself.

Figure 8.8 Tie wire wrapped in loops around millinery wire.

the entire length of tie wire tightly with loops (Figure 8.8), making sure not to make it too bulky.

To join two wires that crisscross each other, cut a 2- or 3-inch piece of tie wire. Center the tie wire right over the cross and wrap the two loose tail ends around the millinery wire. Twist the tie wire onto itself a few times to get a good grip, then wrap the tie wire in an X around the millinery wire cross three or four times. Wrap tightly with constant tension on the tie wire. Leave yourself enough tie wire to twist the ends together to lock the tie wire. Use your needle-nose pliers to make sure the final

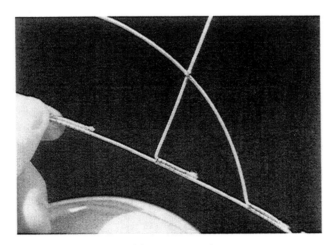

Figure 8.9 Cross joint (above a T-joint).

twists on the tie wire are very snug and strong—but be careful not to snap the wire in half. Remember not to pile up so much wire that you create a lot of bulk. You can make a very strong joint without overwrapping. If there is excess wire remaining after you have made the final twist, cut it off (don't cut off the twists that are holding the wire closed) and tuck the remaining twisted stub around the joint.

Sealing the Tie Wire

Once you have made all your joints and your hat frame is all together, you are ready to permanently fuse all the wires together. A fused-together hat frame will give you a very stable structure that you can easily cover with fabric. It will also hold up better to use and survive most storage conditions better than a frame that isn't fused will. In addition to fusing the joints, I like to seal all of the millinery wire to prevent fraying and to give the wire a surface that accepts paint. I do this with Sculpt Or Coat, a nontoxic plasticized multipurpose coating manufactured for the theatrical industry. It is thick and pasty, and dries clear—or you can add pigment to it if you prefer. Once dry, it accepts spray paint, which makes it ideal for making sheer wire-frame hats—you can paint the frame to match the sheer fabric. To apply Sculpt Or Coat, use your fingers or a brush to coat the millinery wire, thoroughly coating the tie wire joints (Figure 8.10). Apply the Sculpt Or Coat smoothly, leaving no lumps. Sculpt Or Coat

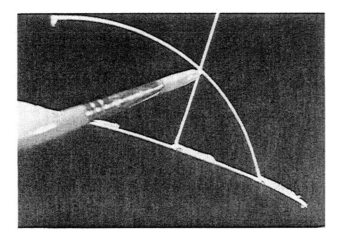

Figure 8.10 Sealing wire joints with Sculpt Or Coat.

comes in large containers, and you shouldn't leave the lid off for too long—it will dry out. Use a small yogurt cup to make a miniature resealable tub for your Sculpt Or Coat. Just be sure to label it so it doesn't accidentally get eaten!

Making the Hat

There are many ways to make a wire-frame hat. It may seem intimidating at first since there is no mold or form to use, but it really can be easy. I usually begin by making the crown and then work my way out to the brim. This project makes a wide-brimmed lady's hat, the kind you might find perched atop a late-Victorian hairstyle. The hat does not fit a typical head size, but has an extra-large round crown to fit around a big hairstyle.

Shaping the Frame

Using the overlapping joint you have learned, make two perfect circles 25 inches around. Remember to check the plane of the wire with the table test. One of these will be the head-size opening of the hat, and the other will be the edge of the tip of the crown. Now make a circle that is 30 inches around. This will be the outside brim edge.

Next, make the straight support cross-pieces that will connect all three circles. Make six identical pieces shaped like the letter L. Straighten the wire with your fingers. One leg of the L should be 2½ inches long and the other should be 5 inches long. Use a ruler and a pencil to mark each piece before bending. Make the bends with needle-nose pliers to get a good sharp corner and give each piece the table test. On the 2½-inch leg, measure from the end of the wire ½ inch and put a mark. Bend the wire at this mark to make a tab that you will use to join the wire to the tip circle (Figure 8.11). Check your tabs with a right angle to make sure they are square.

On each circle, place a pencil mark to indicate the center back. (Usually you will want the center back to be where the wires are joined together.) Measure around each circle starting from the center back mark and mark the halfway point. This is the center front. Measure from the center front to the center back. Divide this distance into thirds and mark the thirds with a pencil. Mark each circle all the way around. Mark all three of your wire circles this way.

Now get all of your parts (Figure 8.12) and we'll start attaching them together. Start with the head-size opening circle (one of the 25-inch circles). Take one of the L shapes and tie it at its corner to the center back mark using tie wire. Tie the cor-

Figure 8.11 L piece with a half-inch tab.

ners of all of the L wires to this circle on the marks. Make sure to orient all of the L's the same (Figure 8.13). Next, wire the crown-tip circle to the bent tabs on the top of the short legs of the L's using the parallel tying method, making sure to line up the center backs of both circles. When you have all of them wired together, place the assembled crown with its sprawling spokes flat on the table to give the whole piece the table test. Make sure it's flat before you proceed (Figure 8.14).

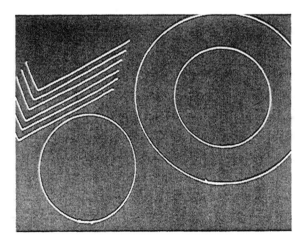

Figure 8.12 Pieces for a wire-frame hat.

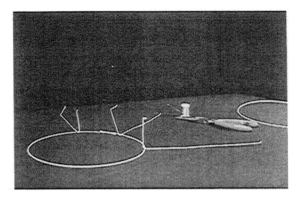

Figure 8.13 L pieces tied to the head-size circle.

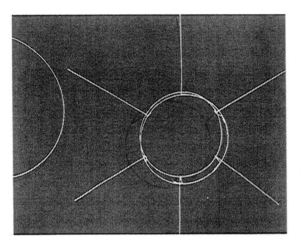

Figure 8.14 Crown circles tied to the tabs on the ends of the L pieces.

Place the outer brim edge on the support spokes of the brim, properly orienting the center back (Figure 8.15). Measure around the hat checking the distance from the head-size opening to the outer brim edge. The goal is to get them all the same. Once you have determined what the distance should be, mark the outer edge on each spoke.

Use your needle-nose pliers to bend a tab on the end of each spoke, paying attention to the plane of the brim. Each tab should be ½ inch but not much longer. Tie the tabs to the outer brim edge on the marks (Figure 8.16).

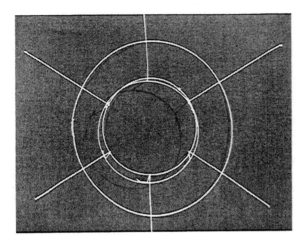

Figure 8.15 Placing the outer brim.

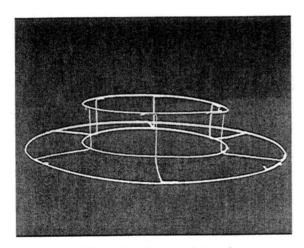

Figure 8.16 Tabs tied to the outer brim edge.

Once the whole thing is together, apply Sculpt Or Coat to the whole thing, making sure all the joints are well covered. Allow to thoroughly dry before painting or covering with fabric.

Covering the Frame

If you are covering a wire frame with sheer fabric, you may want to paint the frame a matching color before proceeding. Paint from all directions to properly cover all areas of the frame. Make sure any paint is completely dry before you begin to work with fabric around the frame. If you've spray painted the hat, air it out before bringing it into close quarters. Paint fumes can give people headaches, nausea, etc. (Read all paint labels and follow all safety instructions.)

Measure across the crown (Figure 8.17) (the diameter) and write this number down. Measure the side of the crown (Figure 8.18) (the height) and multiply by two. Write the resulting number down. Add the two numbers together. Add two seam allowances, or 1¼ inches to that number, assuming a ⅝-inch seam allowance. Add another 1¾ inches for ease. Add all of the numbers to get the diameter of your crown pattern. On brown craft paper, make your pattern with a compass. If your compass doesn't go that big, pin a string in the center of the paper and measure the distance on the string. Holding the string firmly outstretched, rotate it around the pin and use a pencil to mark the appropriate distance until you have marked out the circle.

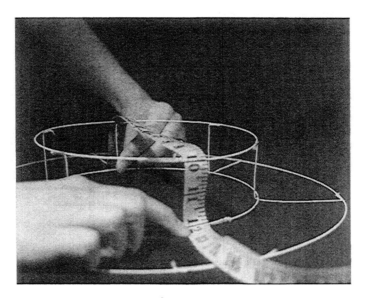

Figure 8.17 Measure across the crown.

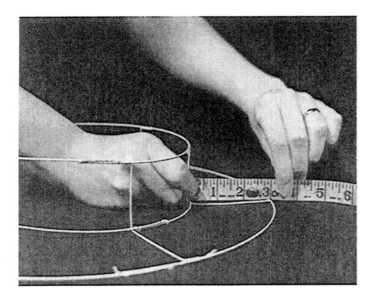

Figure 8.18 Measure across the brim,

We'll next make the pattern for the fabric brim cover, which will be a large rectangle shape. To get the correct dimensions, first measure across the brim. Double
that number and write it down. Add two seam allowances, or 1 ¼ inches. Now add
½ inch for ease. Total your numbers to get the width of the rectangular brim pattern. To determine the length, measure around the outside edge of the wire-frame
brim and write this number down. Add two seam allowances, or 1 ¼ inches, and an
additional 1 inch for ease. Total the numbers to get the length of your brim pattern.
Use these dimensions to draw a rectangle on brown paper. Be sure to label all your
pattern pieces and mark the center front and center back.

Now that you have your pattern made, choose a fabric. I would suggest something
very lightweight, like chiffon. You will need to cut out one brim piece and two
crown pieces (one for the outside and one for the lining). Pin the patterns to the fabric using straight pins, then cut the fabric with your cloth-only scissors.

If your fabric is so thin or flimsy that it is difficult to work with, you can make it
easier to put on the hat by flat-lining the fabric with a piece of tulle or netting in a
matching color. Flat-lining is a process of sewing a layer of underfabric to your fabric in order to stiffen or add body to the fabric. After a flat lining is added to a fabric,

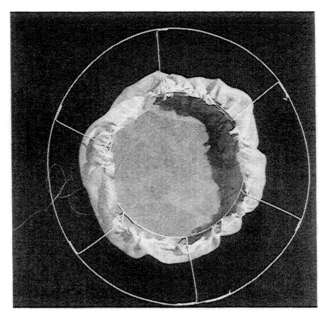

Figure 8.19 Crown fabric gathered onto the wire frame.

both pieces are usually treated as one layer. Once the pieces are cut out, you are ready to cover the hat.

To cover the brim, sew the two short sides of the brim fabric together using a ⅝-inch seam allowance. Make sure to backstitch at the beginning and end of the seam. Press the seam open with a steam iron. Use the sewing machine to run a gathering stitch around both long edges of the brim fabric. Put the stitched fabric around the wire frame, centering it on the outer brim edge. Pin in place (Figure 8.19). Gather one of the gathering stitches on the top of the brim and gather the other on the bottom of the brim. Use a hand-sewing needle and thread to stitch the top and bottom edges together in the seam allowance around the head-size opening.

To cover the crown, run a gathering stitch around the outer edge of the crown fabric in the seam allowance. Place the fabric over the crown and pull the gathering thread. Make sure your seam allowance is tucked under and inside the gathered crown covering. Pin the fabric to the frame (Figure 8.20), then slip stitch the gathered crown fabric to the gathered brim fabric. Remember, you want your stitches to be invisible.

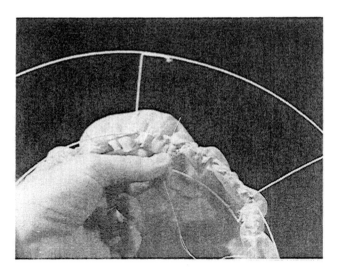

Figure 8.20 Sewing the seam allowance over the wire with a whipstitch.

Next, put a lining in the hat. I have suggested using the second circle we cut out for the lining, but you may use different fabric if you like. On the sewing machine, run a gathering stitch around the outer edge of the lining fabric in the seam allowance. Gather the gathering stitch and place the lining in the hat. Pin it in place, distributing the fullness evenly around the hat. Make sure to tuck the seam allowance under and inside the hat. This will sandwich all of your seam allowances on the hat between the crown and lining fabrics. Hand stitch the lining into the hat. Finish it all off with a grosgrain ribbon around the head-size opening, making sure the center back seam is lined up with the hat's center back.

To finish the hat, put a decorative ribbon around the outside of the crown, perhaps making a bow where the ribbon meets. When you are through, you'll have a strong, well-built, lightweight hat that will perch delicately atop any large hairstyle.

Exercises

1. Make a wire box, a wire cone, and a wire sphere using millinery wire. Make each one small enough to put into a shoe box. Seal all of the wire and joints. Allow them to dry, then paint the shapes.

2. Find pictures of ladies' Victorian hats. Using them as inspiration, decorate your fabric-covered wire-frame hat with feathers and flowers. See how historically accurate you can make the hat look.

3. Make hair-pinning loops for your hat. Get some nylon horsehair braid and cut four 1-inch pieces. Fold each piece in half. One at a time, melt the cut ends together. To do this, hold one folded-in-half braid with your pliers, making sure the two cut edges are lined up with each other. Using a long-stemmed butane lighter (the kind made to light barbecue grills), carefully melt the frayed edges of the horsehair until the two layers fuse together. Be careful not to get the flame near your hands, and don't work near any flammable materials. It is best to do this outside, as long as it isn't windy. Be careful not to set the nylon braid on fire—it won't burn too long, but you don't want to char it. Stitch the loops onto the ribbon inside your hat. Place them at the side fronts and side backs, with the melted end up inside the hat and the smoother folded end sticking out at the bottom. Be sure to leave a slight bit of each horsehair loop sticking out so the wearer can easily find it with a hairpin. With practice, you'll be able to make many horsehair loops effortlessly and quickly.

9
Making Straw
and Felt Hats

Creating a Straw Hat

Although straw is pretty easy to work with, it is usually best when making a straw hat to start with a proven piece of straw that is as close to the desired finished shape as you can find. Whenever possible, I try to use existing straw hats and alter them, or I order a straw body (a piece of straw material) from a millinery supplier. These large dome-shaped pieces are known as *hoods*, *blanks*, or *cartwheels*. These are sold to hat manufacturers to be shaped into finished hats by milliners, and they can be expensive. To learn to work with the material, you might instead shop for an inexpensive large-brim straw hat in the women's accessory department of a department store.

You might encounter straw braid. Many straw hats are made of straw braid, a continuous thin strip of woven straw stitched together in concentric overlapping bands until the desired size and shape is achieved. Hats made of straw braid are more difficult to stretch because of the stitching throughout. You can also purchase straw braid on a spool and use it to make your own hat. To do so, you shape the braid as you stitch it together. Use plenty of steam to help you achieve the shape you need. As you steam and stitch the braid to itself, work the evolving hat over a pressing ham or head block to get a well-shaped hat.

If you are working with an existing straw hat, remove any decorations and hatbands before you start. Also remove any inner head-size ribbons—the purpose of this ribbon is to keep the hat from stretching. Once you have stripped the hat down

Figure 9.1 Various straw hats.

to its basic straw body, you can begin to reshape it. Choose a head block or other form to drape the straw over to reshape it. Pick a shape or size that is a little larger than the head size of the straw body. Keep in mind that straw, like most millinery materials, is not a miracle fabric and it won't stretch to twice its original size. As with buckram, cover the head block completely with plastic wrap to keep it from getting damaged by water.

Straw should be worked with while it is wet. If you try to stretch straw or to shape it when it's dry, you will more than likely break its fibers. Fill a sink or a large pan with warm water and submerge the straw body (Figure 9.2). Soak the straw until it becomes easily pliable. How long this will take depends on how much moisture is in the straw to begin with. Generally, the older the straw, the less moisture will be in it, and the more fragile and easily destroyed it will be. For this exercise, be sure you are working with fairly new straw. You will probably need to soak your hat for at least twenty minutes in warm water. (You can also work straw while infusing it with a lot of steam.)

Once the hat has become saturated, remove it from the water and place it on your plastic-protected head block. Stretch the straw over and around the block until it smoothly covers the form (Figure 9.3). If the hat will not stretch over the shape you

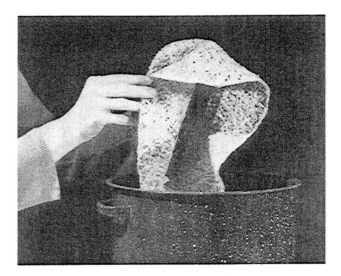

Figure 9.2 Soaking the straw in a pan of warm water.

Figure 9.3 Stretching the wet straw over a form.

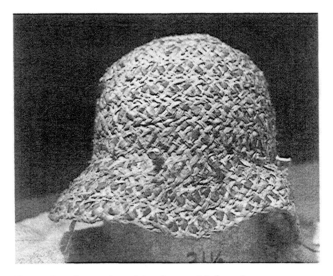

Figure 9.4 Straw pinned in place and left to dry.

have chosen, select a form that is a little smaller and try again. Artificial straw may not stretch as well as real straw. Once the hat is stretched over the form, use a piece of elastic to secure the bottom of the hat snugly to the block. If you need to, use stainless steel pushpins to secure it in place (Figure 9.4). Be sure to put the pins into the open spaces in the straw weave, not through the straw itself, or you'll leave permanent pinholes in the straw.

If you have enough of a brim, turn it up and pin it to the head block (Figure 9.5). You might use another piece of elastic to help pull the straw in at the top of the brim edge.

Allow the straw to dry thoroughly before removing it from the head block. You now have an excellent shape to make a cloche hat.

You might want to trim away some excess straw from the edge of the brim. Be sure to mark the desired new edge before you start cutting. Before you cut, stay stitch the straw. A stay stitch is a straight sewing-machine stitch that prevents material from fraying or stretching. Measure ¼ inch up from the desired edge to find the stay-stitch line. Stay stitch the edge using long stitches. Be sure to backstitch at the beginning and end. Cut the new edge on your straw being careful not to cut through the stitching.

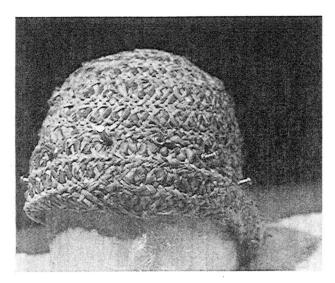

Figure 9.5 Brim rolled up over a roll of fabric and pinned in place to dry.

To finish the raw edge of the straw, iron a grosgrain ribbon into a curve. Fold it in half lengthwise, then press it with a steam iron. Place the ribbon over the cut edge and carefully stitch it to the hat. With practice you will be able to machine stitch this edge ribbon on both sides with only one pass through the sewing machine. If you are not having luck lining up the edges to do this, line up the outside edge of the ribbon and machine stitch only that edge to the hat, then hand stitch the inside edge of the ribbon.

A straw hat needs sizing (stiffening) to keep its shape. After the straw is in the desired shape, put on a layer of sizing. Hat sizing is rather thick, and you may need to thin it a little with hat sizing thinner or lacquer thinner. Hat sizing is quite toxic and flammable: Work in a well-ventilated space and use proper safety precautions. There are several methods you can use to apply the sizing. To get a very hard finish, apply it thickly with a paintbrush (Figure 9.6). Make sure there is no paint residue of any kind in the brush—the chemicals in the sizing will clean the brush and deposit the residue on your hat.

I prefer to apply sizing with pressurized spray bottles (available at hardware stores). These small sprayers come with small clear jars that hold the perfect amount of sizing, and with a charged propellant canister. The spray they emit is fine and

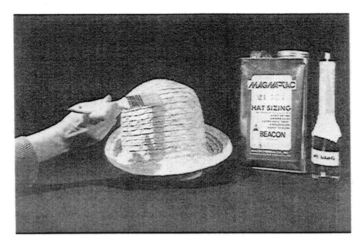

Figure 9.6 Applying hat sizing in a well-ventilated space.

even, and the sprayers aren't too expensive. If you use them, be sure to duct tape the jar and the propellant cartridge together—the chemicals in the sizing tend to eat through the glue that holds the sprayer together.

Figure 9.7 Melanie Starnes-Mortimer in a straw cloche.

Apply the sizing in light coats, allowing it to dry between coats. I like to apply a coat of sizing on the inside of the hat if I need it to be extra sturdy. Be aware that sizing is quite strong and will emit fumes even after it is dry. Apply sizing well in advance of putting the hat on someone's head, or the fumes may give the wearer a headache. Give your hats time to air out.

Exercises

1. Take a new straw hat and take a picture of it as is so that you can have a before-and-after record of your process. Remove all the trimmings, hatbands, etc. This time, reshape the hat using only a steamer. You may also use a steam iron—just make sure the iron is clean so you don't leave muck on the straw. Ironing is useful when you need the straw to go flat. Be careful not to burn your hands with the hot steam. Try to make the hat very noticeably different than it was, concentrating on the brim. If the original brim was flat, turn it up. If the original brim was turned up, flatten it. If you need to, stay stitch and cut the straw. Saturate the straw with steam and hold it in place until it dries. You may want to keep the hat on a head block and use pushpins or elastic to hold it in place until it's dry. Allow the hat to dry completely (usually an hour or two) before removing it from the form.

2. Buy a cheap straw braid hat. Remove all the trimmings, hatbands, etc. and carefully take out the stitches that hold the braid together. Use a steam iron to press the braid flat if it seems to be unruly. See if you can sew the braid into a new shape, stitching the rows on the sewing machine. Use steam to help shape the hat as you go if you need to. If you want to make a really large hat, get two matching cheap straw braid hats, take them both apart, and use both to make one big hat.

3. Find an existing straw hat (perhaps in your costume shop storage) that is not in the best condition and see if you can steam it and reblock it on a head block to freshen it up. Apply a light coat of sizing if it needs one. Retrim the hat and see how good you can make it look.

4. If you have any straw hats that have small tears in them, or that are just getting too fragile to use, make a repair. Get some cheesecloth and use fabric dye to make it closely match the hat's color. Carefully remove all of the

trimmings, hatbands, etc., from the hat and gently clean it with a damp cloth. When the hat has dried, use a brush to coat the inside of the hat with a layer of Sculpt Or Coat. While it is still wet, imbed a layer of the cheesecloth into the Sculpt Or Coat and brush another layer on top. Allow this to dry (perhaps for several hours). If there are tears visible on the outside of the hat, paint the cracks with more Sculpt Or Coat. Don't worry about the color—the Sculpt Or Coat will dry clear. After it has dried thoroughly, redecorate the hat.

Creating a Felt Hat

Once cut, felt edges don't need any other finishing, which allows you to create wonderful, perhaps fanciful, hats (Figures 9.8 and 9.9). Working with felt is similar to working with straw. You can work it by first completely soaking it in warm water and then draping it over a head block or other form, or you can work it by thor-

Figure 9.8 Various felt hats.

Figure 9.9 A new felt hood.

oughly steaming and stretching it. You can also work with felt simply by cutting or folding it and stitching it into place. You may want to stay stitch the edges to prevent stretching or to add decoration.

Like straw, felt usually needs to have a finishing coat of sizing to help keep its shape. I recommend using a spray to apply the sizing. As you apply sizing to some felts, little droplets of sizing may collect on the surface. There are a few ways to deal with this. One way is to use a sweater shaver on the felt before you apply the sizing. These small shavers are used to remove fuzz and balled-up fibers on the surface of sweaters. Another method works well after you have applied the sizing. Once the first coat is dry, lightly sand the hat with fine sandpaper and brush off any residue with a soft brush. Apply another coat. Felt is made of different fibers and sometimes you cannot predict how felt will react to sizing. When you are in doubt about how a felt will react, test using a small scrap of the felt.

Let's try shaping a felt hat with steam. Use either a new felt hood or an old felt hat from which all the trimmings, headbands, etc., have been removed. If the felt has any stay stitching in it, remove the stitches carefully so as not to damage the felt. Don't use felt that has a hole in it, such as a slash where a feather went through the hat. Measure inside the hat to determine the head size and choose a head block that is slightly larger. As with straw, you don't want to try to stretch the felt too much bigger than it is, or you'll run the risk of making the felt too thin, or worse, tearing it. Again, cover your head block with plastic wrap to protect it from the steam and any sizing that might be in the felt.

When working with any fabric, especially felt, it is very important not to overwork the material. Materials that are overworked start to look shabby, wrinkled, soiled, and old. Clean your hands often and don't wad up materials or pile things on them as you work.

Heat up your steamer. When the steam is ready, hold the felt shape over the steam until the crown part is thoroughly saturated (Figure 9.10). Be careful not to burn yourself with the steam. You'll need to move the hat around to ensure that all parts are steamed properly. Before too much steam escapes, put the felt on your head block. Using some muscle, grab the bottom edge and pull it down onto the form (Figure 9.11). If it doesn't slide down onto the head block, you may be trying to

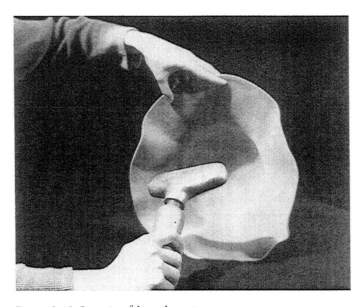

Figure 9.10 Steaming felt to shape it.

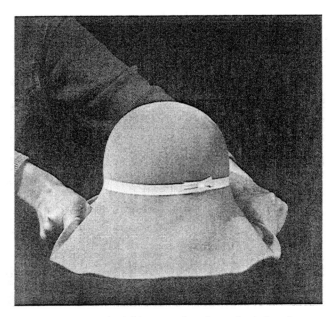

Figure 9.11 Stretched felt secured with an elastic band.

stretch the felt too much at one time. Choose a smaller head block and try again. If you need to stretch the hat substantially larger, you can gradually stretch it over larger and larger blocks. The felt should slide down (at least mostly) onto the head block. Pick up the head block with the felt on it and hold it over the steam, being sure to steam the crown anywhere that it seems to be resisting stretching. When the fabric is saturated with steam, put the block back on the table and try pulling the felt down onto it again. Keep repeating this process until you have the felt smoothed all the way down on the head block. You may want to tie an elastic band around the bottom to hold it in place until it dries thoroughly. I avoid putting pushpins into felt crowns since they leave perforations in the hat.

When the hat is dry (usually several hours later), remove it from the head block. Trim the felt into any shape desired. You may wish to machine stay stitch the head-size opening to prevent further stretching.

Often you will find it easier to make a felt hat in two sections from two matching pieces of felt, stretching the crown first, then attaching the brim. In this method, be sure to leave yourself a seam allowance of at least ⅝ inch inside the brim head-size opening. Clip all around so that you have seam allowance tabs all around the opening in the brim. These tabs can be folded up into the crown and stitched to the crown.

Another method to make a crown and brim requires a head block that will work in conjunction with a brim block. This is how many men's hats are manufactured, including fedoras and bowlers. First stretch the felt over a head block. Then place the brim block over the head block and felt—it's like putting a peg into a hole. Once the brim block is positioned, stretch the remaining felt up and around the brim block using plenty of steam. Secure the edges of the felt with elastic or pushpins (use pins only if you have a little edge to pin through that you can trim away later). Once the felt is dry, remove the elastic, pins, and blocks and apply sizing.

To finish a felt hat, stitch a grosgrain ribbon around the inside head-size opening. Often this can be done on a sewing machine. Be sure to put the ribbon's seam at the center back of the hat, even though the crown may not have a center back seam. Some felt hats may need a lining. Most felt hats have a ribbon band around the outside. The ribbons on women's hats can be just about any color, but men's hats traditionally have a ribbon that is the same color as or darker than the felt.

Exercises

1. This exercise works best with thick good-quality felt. Go to a hardware store and purchase a couple of small shallow stairrail finials or large decorative cabinet knobs. Tape them in place on top of your head block and try stretching felt over them to create a decorative bump on top of a felt crown. See how intricate a shape you can achieve. You can use clay sculpting tools to press the felt into crevices and indentations—just make sure the tools are new or very clean so you don't ruin the felt. You may need to wrap elastic bands around the felt to pull it in tightly against the form—use steam to help get a better fit.

2. Try stretching soaked felt over three shapes, a square, a sphere, and a pointy cone. Which is easier, and why?

3. Stretch a felt hood over a head block and hold it in place with an elastic band. Get some clean extra-thick rope or cording and wrap it with plastic wrap. Wrap the rope around where you put the elastic band. Stretch the felt up over the rope and fasten with another elastic band. Use your hands and plenty of steam to smooth the felt over the rope or cording. This creates a turned-up

brim. When the hat has dried, remove it from the block. Add sizing and trimmings to finish the hat.

4. You might need extra reinforcement on the brim of a felt hat in order to achieve the desired shape. Try zigzagging a wire to the edge of a felt brim. The wire should be right on the edge of the felt—not on the top or underneath (Figure 9.12). Next, cover the wire with a strip of bias-cut fabric. (Choose a fairly thin material for good results.) Straight stitch the fabric in place, and remember to fold the beginning edge under as you sew (Figure 9.13). After you have sewn the bias fabric all the way around the brim, fold the fabric over the edge of the brim, covering the wire. You can finish the edging by hand-sewing the other side of the bias fabric edge band to the hat (or if you are skilled at using the sewing machine, you can machine stitch it in place). After it is stitched in place, lightly press the new edge band with a steam iron to give it a crisp finished look (Figure 9.14).

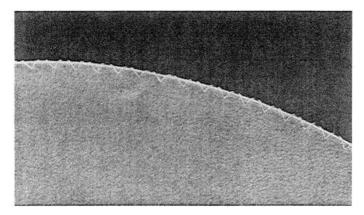

Figure 9.12 Wire zigzagged onto the edge of the brim.

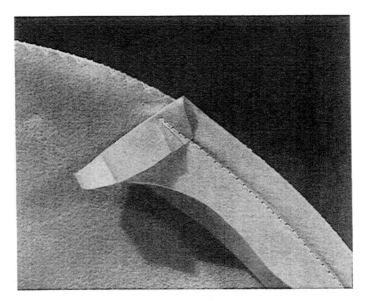

Figure 9.13 Covering the wire with a bias strip.

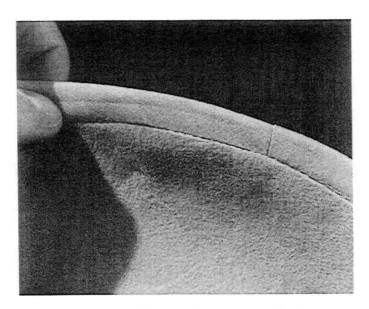

Figure 9.14 Bias strip folded over the edge and stitched to secure.

Glossary

These terms are common in millinery, sewing, and costume construction.

backstitch: When sewing in one direction, you make a few stitches in the opposite direction to lock the stitching in place and prevent unraveling. On a sewing machine, a backstitch is usually done with a lever or button that makes the machine sew in reverse.

back tack: Same as backstitch.

barge cement: A strong contact cement used to glue leather.

bandeau: A crescent- or wedge-shaped flat piece that is inserted under a hat so that when it is on the head, it will tip up on one side or in the back.

beading wire: A thin inexpensive metal wire used to tie millinery wire together.

belting ribbon: Same as French belting.

blank: See *hood*.

bridal glue: A clear strong glue that contains acetone.

brim: The part of a hat that extends from the bottom of the crown at the head-size opening, shading the wearer's face.

buckram: A stiff woven fabric that has been impregnated with water-soluble sizing.

capeline: See *cartwheel*.

cartwheel: An unfinished and unshaped hat body that has a rough dome shape. Cartwheels generally have a wider brim area than capelines. Both are flatter than hoods.

cast: (1) The entire group of actors in a play. (2) A mold taken of an actor's face or other body part, usually done for special makeup effects.

casting: The process of assigning actors to roles in a play.

CB: Shorthand for "center back."

CF: Shorthand for "center front."

chin strap: A strap of fabric or other material that goes from one side of a hat to the other under the chin to keep the hat on the head.

cockade: A geometric rosette of folded ribbon used to adorn the outside of a hat.

cool-melt glue: See *hot-melt glue.*

coque feather: Iridescent feathers, often with a blackish-green sheen.

costume accessories: See *costume crafts.*

costume crafts: Accessory items of theatrical costume that are not made on a sewing machine, such as shoes, hats, armor, belts, and jewelry.

costume designer: The person who makes the ultimate decisions about the costumes in a production.

costume props: See *costume crafts.*

crafts: See *costume crafts.*

craftsperson: In the theater, a person who specializes in costume crafts.

craft scissors: Sturdy scissors that are designated for use on paper, buckram, and other nonfabric materials.

crown: The part of a hat that covers the top of the head.

draper: A person who makes patterns for garments.

draping: In costuming, the art and craft of making patterns for garments.

dressmaking shears: Very sharp scissors specially made to cut fabric.

dress rehearsal: A complete run-through of a play without an audience, in which actors wear their costumes.

ease: The practice in pattern making of adding extra fullness to garments to allow the wearer more room for movement.

fitting: A time to get an actor to try on a costume or costume parts to determine the size and fit, and to consider aesthetic issues before the costumes are used in rehearsal.

flat-lining: A stiffening layer of fabric sewn to a thinner outer fabric. Both layers, once joined, are treated as one layer.

foundation: In millinery, the understructure of a hat, usually made of buckram, wire, or other stiff material, over which fabric is stretched or draped to create the finished hat.

French belting: A high-quality grosgrain ribbon that can be easily ironed into a curve.

French curve: A drawing aid—a flat tool that is a collection of various arcs and curves used to draw rounded lines and shapes.

front-to-back: The head measurement that goes from the front of the forehead to the back of the head across the top of the head.

Fuller's earth (or Fuller's chalk): A special powdered clay substance used to clean hats.

glycerin: An oily fluid good for conditioning feathers and for creating faux sweat stains around a hatband.

grosgrain ribbon: A fabric band that is woven with raised ribs. If made of cotton (or mostly cotton) it will iron into a curve. Also see *French belting*.

hairline measurement: A measurement taken around a person's hairline, starting at the center front of the forehead and ending at the base of the skull.

ham: See *pressing tools*.

hat size: The size of a hat, or the industry standard guide for determining that size. (See chart on p. 17.)

hatter: See *milliner.*

hat band: A ribbon or fabric strip that encircles the outside of a hat around the base of the crown.

hatmaker: See *milliner.*

hat pin: A long, sharp straightpin, often with a decorative head, used to secure a hat to the wearer's hair.

hat sizing: A liquid that is brushed or sprayed onto fabric or a hat to make it stiffer and add stability and strength. Also called *hat lacquer.*

head block: A carved wooden form, available in different sizes, that approximates the shape and size of the human head.

headshot: An actor's standard photograph, often in black and white, that's sent with the actor's résumé to casting agents.

head size: The measurement around the head above the eyebrows, where a hat usually sits.

head-size opening: The hole in a hat that sits right above the eyebrows and the ears around the head.

head-size ribbon: A band sewn to the inside of a hat around the head-size opening.

hood: An unfinished wide cone shape made of felt or straw intended to be further shaped by a milliner. Also called a *blank.*

horsehair braid: A sheer flexible flat nylon braid. Available in various widths.

hot-melt or cool-melt glue gun: A trigger-operated gunlike appliance that accepts premade glue sticks, melts them, and emits a continuous stream of glue that hardens as it cools. Once cool, the glue is not tacky.

interfacing: A layer of material used to back fabric to increase its stiffness.

lacquer: See *hat sizing.*

lining: A fabric layer inside a hat that protects both the hat and the wearer's hairstyle.

material safety data sheet (MSDS): Written information compiled by chemical manufacturers to inform a user about a product's properties and hazards.

milliner: A specially skilled craftsperson who patterns, makes, and decorates hats and other hair ornaments and head garments.

millinery glue: See *bridal glue.*

millinery needles: Hand-sewing needles that are long, strong, and sharp, yet flexible.

millinery wire: A cloth- or thread-covered wire used for hat construction. It is available in various gauges.

mock-up: A basic facsimile of a hat, made of inexpensive materials to approximate the size and scale of a hat. A mock-up can usually be taken apart and used as a pattern.

mull: A thin fabric used as an underlayer to soften hard edges. Also called *mulling.*

muslin: A plain-weave inexpensive cotton fabric, available in different thicknesses.

needle board: A special pressing tool that protects the pile of a fabric (such as velvet) as you iron it from the back side.

needle-nose pliers: A hand tool with thin pointed gripping teeth, good for getting into tight places and for detail work.

offstage: In the theater, literally not on the stage. Usually refers to the space that's immediately behind or beside the stage and out of sight of the audience.

onstage: In the theater, literally on the stage.

overlock sewing machine: A sewing machine that cuts a clean edge on fabric and sews a chain of multiple threads all around the fresh edge to prevent fraying. Some overlock machines also sew a straight stitch beside the overlock stitches for extra security. Also called a *serger.*

pattern: In costume construction, a piece of paper or fabric in the basic shape of part of a finished garment. Pattern pieces are usually labeled and include written instructions for assembling the garment.

pillbox hat: A basic head covering consisting of a sideband and a tip.

pinking shears: Fabric shears with serrated blades that cut fabric with a zigzag edge to deter fraying.

plait: Same as *braid*.

presser foot: The part of a sewing machine that holds the fabric down while the needle goes through the fabric.

pressing ham: See *pressing tools*.

pressing tools: Specially built forms used to maintain the shape of a piece of fabric while it's being ironed.

quilting ruler: A clear plastic ruler marked out in a grid.

rendering: A visual representation of how a finished costume should appear. Usually a drawing, painting, or collage.

scissors: In costume shops, these cutting devices are often assigned to specific jobs and referred to by the job: "fabric-only scissors," "craft scissors," "paper scissors."

seam gauge: A small pattern-making ruler used to measure and add seam allowances.

seam ripper: A small hand tool with a tiny curved blade at the end; used to remove stitches from fabric without damaging it.

serger: See *overlock sewing machine*.

shears: See *scissors*.

sideband: The part of a hat that circles the head and supports the tip on top and the brim on the bottom edge.

side-to-side: The head measurement that goes from just above the ear on one side of the head to just above the ear on the other side of the head, starting and stopping at the head-size measurement line.

sizing: See *hat sizing*.

steamer: An appliance that creates a large volume of steam. Usually has a hose or long nozzle that lets the user direct the steam to specific areas. Used in constructing hats and other costume garments.

straight stitch: Sewing a single line of stitches in a straight row.

tailoring: The art and craft of making patterns for, cutting, fitting, and sewing intricately structured garments.

tailor's points: Very short, very sharp specialty scissors.

tape measure: A long narrow fabric ruler.

tin snips: A scissors-like tool used to cut sheets of tin or other thin metal.

tip: The top-most flat part of a hat that covers the top of the wearer's head.

trim: (1) Noun: Materials used to decorate a costume item. (2) Verb: To apply decoration.

United States Institute for Theatre Technology (USITT): An association of theatrical artists, technicians, suppliers, and managers.

Victorian: From the time of England's Queen Victoria, loosely used to describe the entire nineteenth century.

Bibliography

Albruzio, Ann, Osnat Lustig, and Ted Morrison (photographer). 1998. *Classic Millinery Techniques: A Complete Guide to Making & Designing Today's Hats*. Asheville, NC: Lark Books.

Amphlett, Hilda. 1974. *Hats: A History of Fashion in Headwear*. Chalfont St. Giles, England: Richard Sadler, Ltd.

Anlezark, Mildred. 1993. *Hats on Heads: The Art of Creative Millinery*. Berkeley, CA: Lacis.

Clark, Fiona. 1982. *Hats. The Costume Accessories Series*. New York: Drama Book Publishers.

Dreher, Denise. 1981. *From the Neck Up: An Illustrated Guide to Hatmaking*. Minneapolis, MN: Madhatter Press.

Ingham, Rosemary, and Liz Covey. 1992. *The Costume Technician's Handbook*. Portsmouth, NH: Heinemann.

Notes

Notes

Notes

Notes

Notes

Notes